AF575692

The Beginner's Guide to Brush Lettering

An Interactive Workbook for Creating Beautiful Art

Amy Latta

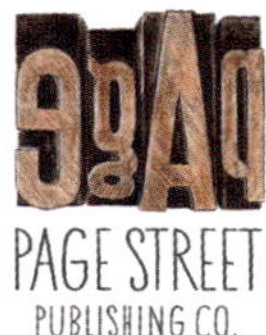

PAGE STREET
PUBLISHING CO.

DEDICATION

For you, dear reader. You have taken the step of opening this book in the hopes of learning a new creative skill. Whether you are confident or completely unsure of your success, you are stepping out and beginning a journey with me. For that, I am grateful. Thank you for trusting me to teach you that you (yes, you!) can brush-letter beautiful things. Let's get started!

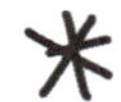

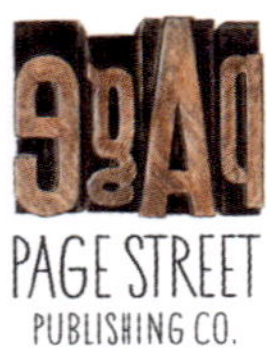

First published in 2023 by
Page Street Publishing Co.
27 Congress Street, Suite 1511
Salem, MA 01970
www.pagestreetpublishing.com

Distributed by Macmillan, sales in Canada by The Canadian Manda Group.

27 26 25 24 23 1 2 3 4 5

ISBN-13: 978-1-64567-969-1
ISBN-10: 1-64567-969-1

Cover and book design by Amy Latta and Meg Baskis for Page Street Publishing Co.
Illustrations by Amy Latta

Printed and bound in China

Page Street Publishing protects our planet by donating to nonprofits like The Trustees, which focuses on local land conservation.

Contents

Introduction — 4

Chapter 1
Brush Technique — 8

Chapter 2
The 8 Basic Brushstrokes — 11

Chapter 3
The Brush Script Alphabet — 18

Chapter 4
Brush Script Lettering — 43

Chapter 5
Flourishes — 47

Chapter 6
Extended Brush Script — 60

Chapter 7
Outlined Brush Script — 73

Chapter 8
Adding Bounce — 75

Beyond the Basics
Bonus Ideas — 81

PROJECTS

1: Live a Life You Love — 84

2: Practice Makes Progress — 88

3: This Is Us — 93

4: Embrace the Journey — 98

5: The Best Is Yet to Come — 102

6: It Is Well With My Soul — 105

7: Coffee Time — 109

8: Always Give Thanks — 113

9: No Rain, No Flowers — 117

10: Do More Than Just Exist — 122

11: Every Moment Matters — 126

12: You Are My Favorite Person — 130

13: Always Be Kind — 134

14: Life Is Short, Eat Dessert First — 138

15: Creative Minds Are Rarely Tidy — 142

16: Alexa, Fold the Laundry — 146

17: This Is My Happy Place — 150

18: Love You to the Moon & Back — 154

19: Feed Me & Tell Me I'm Pretty — 158

20: A Group of People Is Called a "No Thanks" — 162

Afterword — 165
About the Author — 165
Acknowledgments — 166
Index — 167

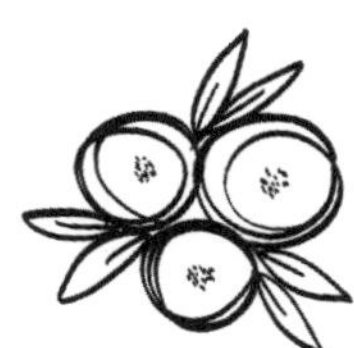

Introduction

If I were stranded on a deserted island and could only bring one thing with me . . . it wouldn't be a brush pen. It would be a private jet so I could go home! However, if I were to find myself with some spare time, whether in a cabana by the pool, in a boring meeting or at the airport waiting on a delayed flight, a brush pen would be my art supply of choice to occupy my time. In the seven years since I first learned to use a brush pen, I have created art in all of those places—and just about everywhere else you can imagine. I've lettered at 10,000 feet in the air, as well as halfway around the world on a trip to China. Wherever I am, as long as I have some paper and a brush pen, I can make art . . . and so can you!

Hand lettering is the process of turning your handwritten words into art. One of the primary tools we use to make that happen is the brush pen. While "hand lettering" encompasses a variety of font styles and embellishments, the most popular style of writing is known as "brush script". What makes brush script unique is that each individual letter contains a combination of thick parts and thinner parts. This contrast is quite aesthetically pleasing, which has made this type of lettering very popular over the last decade. Brush script is what we usually mean when we talk about "brush lettering."

Creating true brush script/brush lettering is indeed an art form. It involves applying and releasing pressure on your brush pen as you write, and it takes practice and repetition to master. The great news, though, is that it's not nearly as difficult to learn as it seems! We're going to start at the very beginning, learning the basic brushstrokes and practicing the building block shapes that we'll combine to create all the letters of the alphabet. Then, we'll move on to connecting our letters and adding fun effects like bounce to take our lettering to the next level.

In this workbook, you'll find instruction, practice space and tons of traceable pages you can use to help you along your lettering journey. Join me as we learn to master the brush pen and discover what it can do.

WHAT IS A BRUSH PEN?

So, what exactly is this magical tool? A brush pen is simply a marker or pen with a flexible tip that is meant to mimic a paintbrush. Unlike an actual brush, where the head is made up of many individual bristles, a brush pen has a solid but flexible tip that moves as a unit. When you apply pressure to it, it bends, causing a larger portion of the tip to make contact with your paper. This, in turn, creates a dark, thick line. If you release that pressure, less of the tip touches the paper, and your markings will be lighter and thinner.

TYPES OF INKS

Brush pens (also known as brush markers) come in a variety of sizes and colors, and they can contain one of several types of ink. Understanding the ink types and how they work will help you choose the best tools for your art projects. Basically, ink is composed of two important parts: color and solvent (a carrier medium that the color is mixed with). Color can come from either dyes or pigments, and the solvent will be either water or alcohol. The way these parts are combined gives us several different types of brush pens, each with its own benefits and drawbacks.

Water is obviously a great choice as a solvent. It is very absorbent and it's nontoxic. Typically, water-based markers are washable and easy to clean up if they get on your hands, clothing or work area. This type of ink works well on porous surfaces, especially paper.

Alcohol acts very differently than water when the ink is applied to a surface. The alcohol evaporates quickly, leaving just the color behind. This makes it very easy to apply multiple layers of color on top of each other without tearing or causing damage to your paper. It is also permanent and works on both porous and nonporous surfaces, making it a great choice for artwork on wood, plastic, metal, fabric and more.

One thing to note about alcohol-based ink is that, because the alcohol evaporates, the color of the ink may look one way when you apply it and change as it dries. For this reason, I always recommend "swatching" your markers. Create a page full of small squares and color in each box with a different marker. Above the box, write the color number or name of the specific marker you used. This way, you will have a reference for what each color looks like when dry so you can choose a palette you love.

Here is a quick reference chart showing the different features of these two types of ink:

WATER-BASED INK	ALCOHOL-BASED INK
Washable with soap and water	Permanent
Works on porous surfaces only (paper)	Works on both porous and nonporous surfaces
Nontoxic	Contains chemicals that can be toxic
Less expensive	More expensive
Layering can tear/pill paper	Great for layering and blending without damaging paper

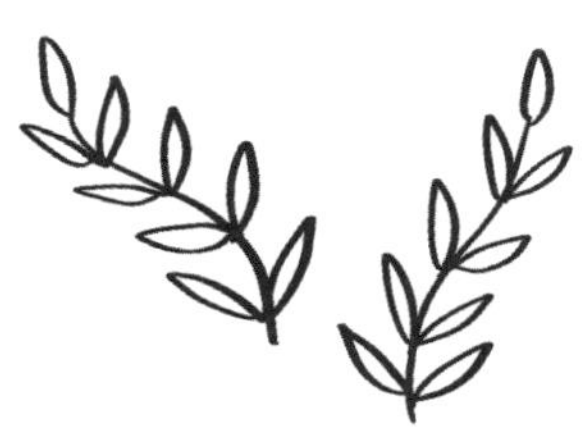

THE THREE MOST COMMON BRUSH PENS

Now, let's look at the three main types of brush pens/markers. If you're wondering which type your favorite markers are, a quick look at the barrel and/or the packaging should help you identify it quickly.

PIGMENT/WATER-BASED

My favorite lettering pen, the Tombow® Fudenosuke, falls into this category. The word "fudenosuke" (FOO-DEN-OH-SOO-KAY) is a Japanese term meaning "a brush that helps." Whether you prefer the soft or hard tip (both are still quite flexible), this is a great pen for small- to medium-size lettering projects. Because the ink is pigment-based, it is mostly waterproof and will not bleed. This attribute will be important for projects like lettering on a watercolor background or using a watercolor effect inside a doodle drawn with this pen. However, it is not permanent and is best suited for paper projects only.

DYE/WATER-BASED

There are many brands and styles of this type of marker on the market, but my favorites are Tombow Dual Brush Pens. Available in 108 colors, these markers have a large brush tip on one end and a small bullet tip on the other. Because of the dye and water combination, when this ink gets wet, you can create all kinds of fun watercolor effects and basically paint with your markers. These are great for lettering, doodling, watercolor and more on paper surfaces.

DYE/ALCOHOL-BASED

These are a favorite choice for many professional artists because of their permanence and the ability to create projects on many kinds of surfaces. Copic®, Spectrum Noir™, Caliart® and Prismacolor® are a few well-known alcohol marker brands. Personally, I like using Tombow ABT PRO Alcohol-Based Markers. One end is, of course, a brush tip and the other end has a chisel tip that's great for drawing lines and creating patterns. These waterproof markers are amazing for blending, for coloring and for projects that need to dry quickly.

BRUSH PEN CARE AND STORAGE

Like any tool, brush pens need to be well cared for in order to continually produce optimal results. Of course, over time, they will experience normal wear and tear from being used, but there are two main things you can do to help keep your brush pens in great condition.

SURFACES

First, protect the tips by using the correct types of papers and surfaces. Using low-quality printer paper for practice is the fastest way to ruin a marker because it will soak up a lot of ink and can even cause the tip to fray. Instead, for water-based markers, opt for high-quality laser printer paper or a smooth, medium-weight sketchbook. For projects, look for something a little heavier and very smooth, like Bristol board. If you'd like to work with watercolor paper, make sure it's hot press, which is smooth to the touch, rather than the textured cold press paper we typically associate with watercolor painting.

Alcohol-based markers work best on Bristol board, hot press watercolor paper or a marker pad. While they can be used on other types of surfaces, make sure those surfaces are smooth to the touch. For example, if you are drawing on a wood slice, sand it as well as possible first or it will do some serious damage to your pens.

STORAGE

One of the most important ways to protect our markers happens when we aren't using them! The way we store a pen actually makes a huge difference. Because many brush pens are dual-tipped—with a brush tip on one end and a bullet or chisel tip on the other—the best way to store them is horizontally. This keeps the ink from pooling at either end and leaving the other one dried out.

Personally, I have a tool cubby similar to what you'd see as a marker display in the craft store and I've arranged my markers inside it by color. Some other options are to store them horizontally in drawers and even to keep them in their original packaging, with one pack stacked on top of another.

Single-tip markers should be stored either upside down or horizontally. When you treat your markers well, they will return the favor and last longer, giving you better quality results.

DIGITAL BRUSH LETTERING

In addition to using physical brush pens, you can also use the techniques in this book to letter digitally. In this case, the Apple® Pencil becomes a substitute for the brush pen, and although the tip doesn't actually flex, it responds to the amount of pressure you apply to it just like a brush pen would. In order to create high-quality digital brush lettering, you'll need an Apple Pencil, any version of iPad® that is compatible with it and an inexpensive app called Procreate®. While there may be other tablets, digital pencils and apps available, Procreate, the Apple Pencil and an iPad are—in my experience and research—the best for digital lettering.

Now that we've covered the basics about brush pens, it's time to put these wonderful little tools to work and start creating some lettering and artwork.

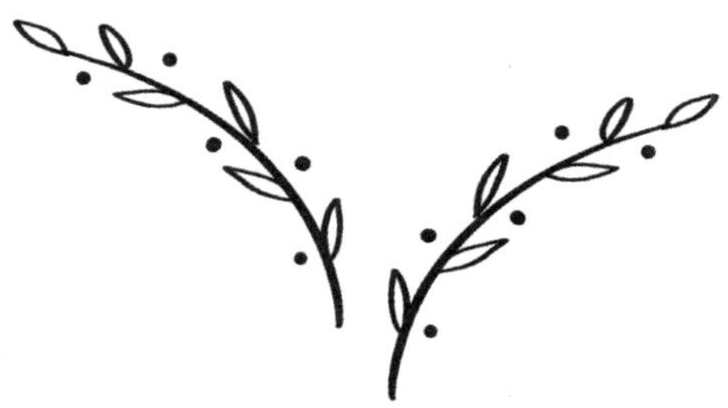

CHAPTER 1

Brush Technique

The quality that makes a brush pen so unique is its ability to respond to the amount of pressure we apply to the tip. When we press on it, the tip flexes and a large portion of it touches the paper, creating a thick line. When we use a light touch, the line becomes thinner, as less of the marker comes in contact with the page. With that in mind, the key to proper brush technique is knowing when to apply pressure and when to release it.

Anytime we write or draw, our pen is moving across the paper in one of three basic directions. It's either moving up away from us (an upstroke), down toward us (a downstroke) or horizontally/diagonally across the page (a horizontal stroke).

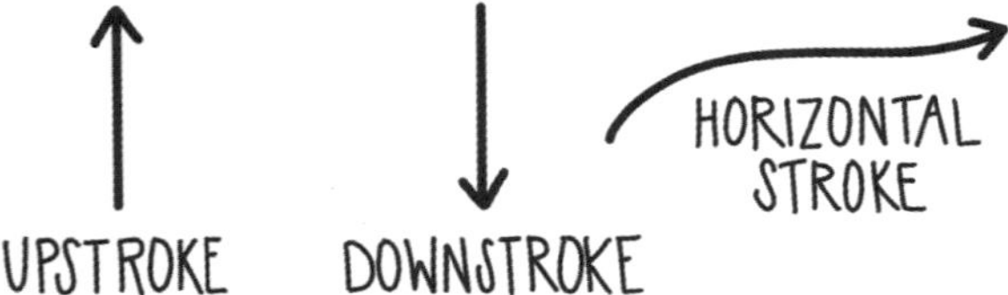

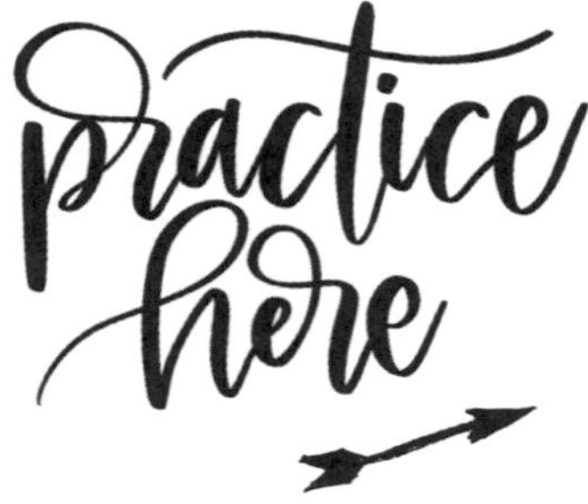

The basic "rule" for proper brush technique is that downstrokes are thick, while everything else remains thin. So, as we write, we apply pressure on every downstroke and release the pressure as soon as our pen begins moving in a different direction. This is what gives brush lettering its characteristic look; within every letter, there is a combination of thick and thin lines.

Now that we know the rule, it's time to start practicing the different types of strokes. Grab any brush pen and some smooth practice paper or, even better, you can practice right here on the page with me. First, we'll start with some downstrokes. Each time you pull the pen toward yourself, apply some pressure to create a dark, thick line. Don't be afraid to press—this is what your pen is made to do! You won't break the tip, I promise.

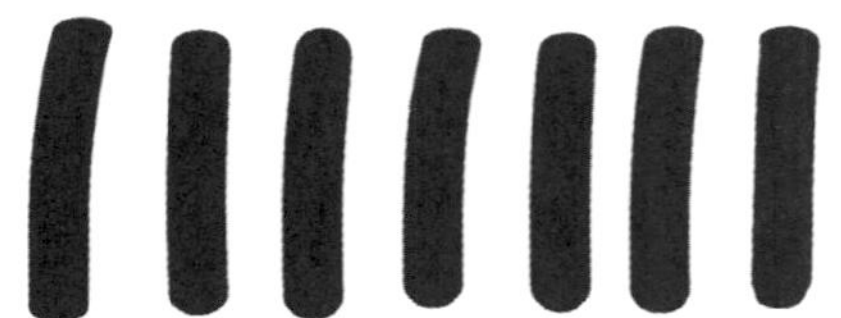

Next, let's try a series of upstrokes. For this, we're going to release the pressure and just let the pen glide on the surface very lightly. You should see a noticeable difference between the thickness of these upstrokes and the downstrokes you created in the previous step.

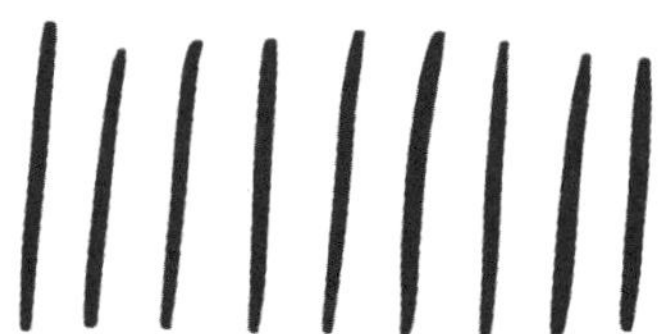

practice here

Feel free to do as many practice strokes as you'd like to get comfortable with this technique. Then, we are going to move on to the next step, which is alternating them. Since you'll be changing the amount of pressure you apply every time your pen changes directions, we're going to practice getting your hand to switch between the two strokes. Make a downstroke, followed by an upstroke and repeat to get a feel for applying and releasing pressure as you go.

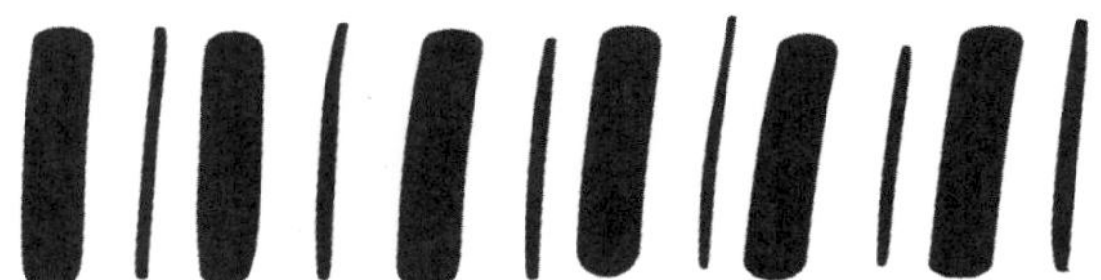

Take your time practicing in the space provided and use the traceable practice sheet on the next page. There's no rush to move on until you feel comfortable with this part, but I think you'll find that you're getting the hang of it pretty quickly. Remember, it doesn't have to be perfect!

PRO TIP: *If you feel like your strokes are shaky, try making them faster and smaller. The larger you write, the more time your hand has to move where you don't want it to go. In the same way, if you're concentrating hard and taking your time, that just gives your hand more time to shake.*

See? Brush technique isn't impossible! It just takes practice and repetition to master. Like biking, driving or anything else our bodies do, it will eventually become muscle memory.

Once you've mastered upstrokes and downstrokes, it's time for the next step. Our goal is to create a brush script alphabet, but of course we can't do that with only straight lines. In order to write the letters, we need to apply brush technique to the eight basic shapes that compose them. Once we do, we can put those shapes together to form everything from A to Z.

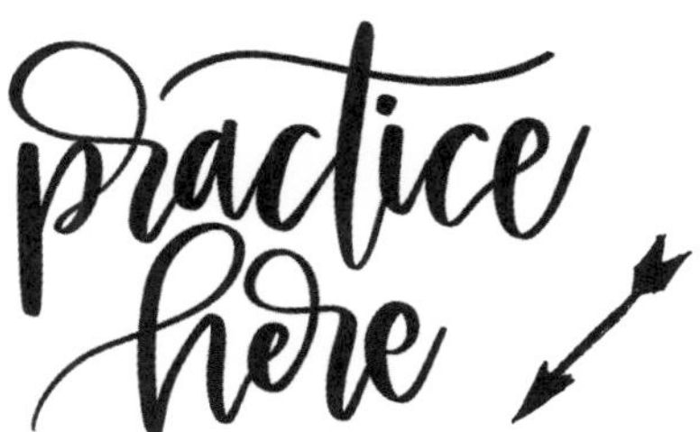

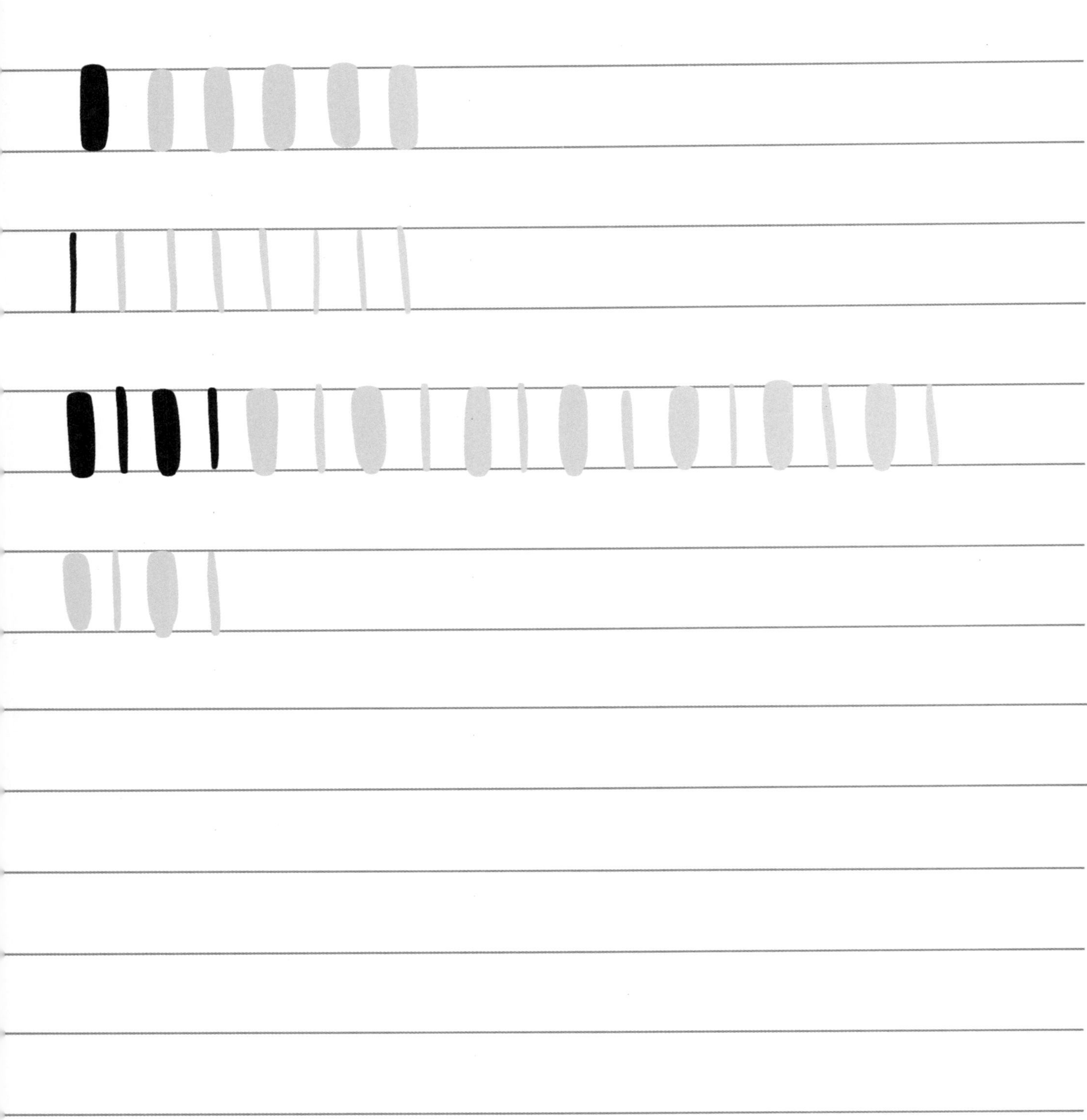

CHAPTER 2

The 8 Basic Brushstrokes

The most common reason I hear from people about why they don't think they can hand letter or brush letter is "I have terrible handwriting." Maybe you fall into that category and your writing is usually not so legible, but don't worry, I have great news! The way we approach hand lettering is not the same as regular handwriting at all. Instead of thinking in terms of whole letters, we're going to break each letter down into a combination of simple strokes. For example, the letter "a" is composed of an oval and an underturn, both of which we'll be learning in this chapter. Once you have practiced the eight basic brushstrokes, you'll be able to combine them to form letters, which then come together to form beautiful brush-lettered words. Grab your favorite brush pen and join me as we tackle these shapes.

UPSTROKE AND DOWNSTROKE

Congratulations! You've already learned two of the eight basic brushstrokes! In the previous chapter, you practiced them individually and alternating. This is the foundation of everything we do with a brush pen, so it's important to feel comfortable with these two strokes. Now, we're going to do something similar, but without lifting our pen in between!

OVERTURN

An overturn is a combination of an upstroke and a downstroke that you draw without lifting your pen from the paper. It resembles an upside-down "u" and I like to think of it as a little hill or mountain. To draw it, you'll move your pen up, over with a curving motion, then down. Just like before, keep the pressure light at first, then press harder as soon as your pen starts moving down toward you.

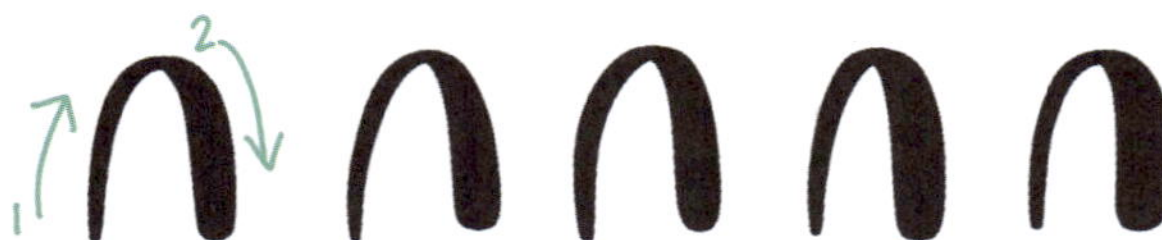

Use the space below to practice. Remember, practice makes progress, so the more you repeat this stroke, the better you'll get at creating it. Then, we'll take a look at the opposite of the overturn: the underturn.

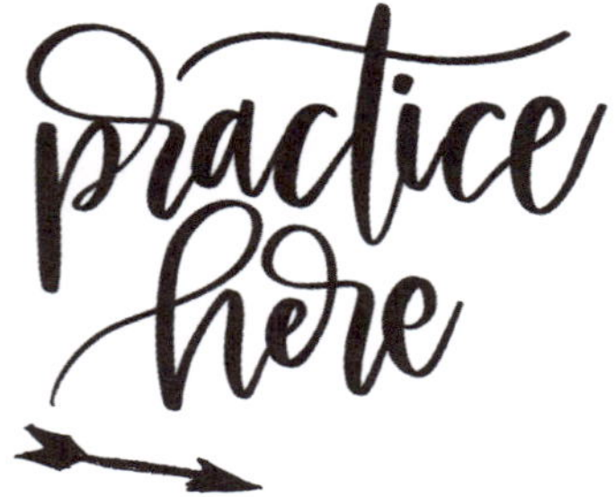

UNDERTURN

An underturn is basically a horseshoe shape. If an overturn is a mountain, the underturn is a valley. It's formed by making a downstroke followed by an upstroke without picking up your pen. As your pen moves down, you'll apply pressure, then as soon as your pen starts moving to the side, you'll release that pressure, moving the pen over and up.

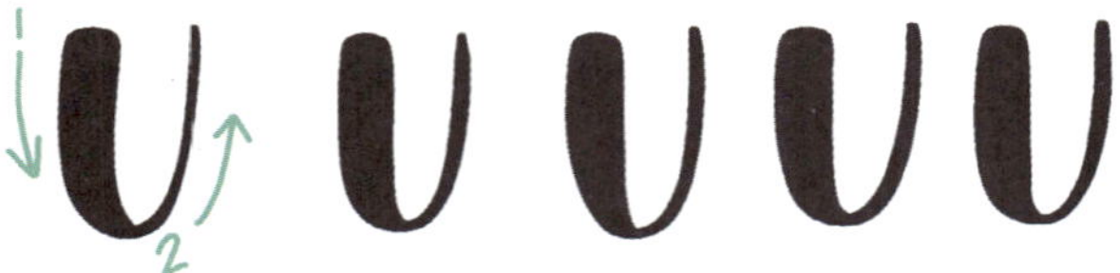

The trickiest part of this shape is the transition at the bottom. Take a look at the examples below. You'll see that if you release the pressure too soon or too late, the shape won't look quite right. Try releasing the pressure gradually rather than suddenly for a smooth transition.

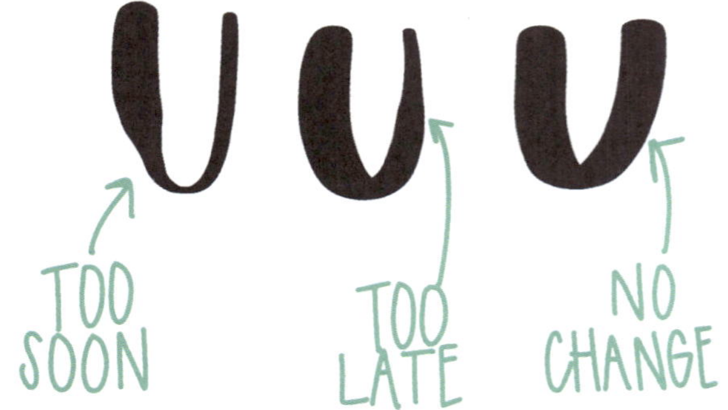

Take some time in the space below to practice making underturns.

Sometimes, when we use this shape in a letter, the right side (the upstroke) doesn't go all the way back up to the top. Try making some underturns where the right side only goes up about halfway as high as the downstroke. Then, when you feel ready, go ahead and move on to the next brushstroke.

COMPOUND CURVE

When we combine the overturn and the underturn, we get something called a compound curve. Basically, this is the technical term for a squiggle. To form this shape, you'll begin with an upstroke, then switch to a downstroke and finally back to an upstroke. Practicing this compound curve will help you get the hang of repeatedly changing how much pressure you apply to the pen as you write.

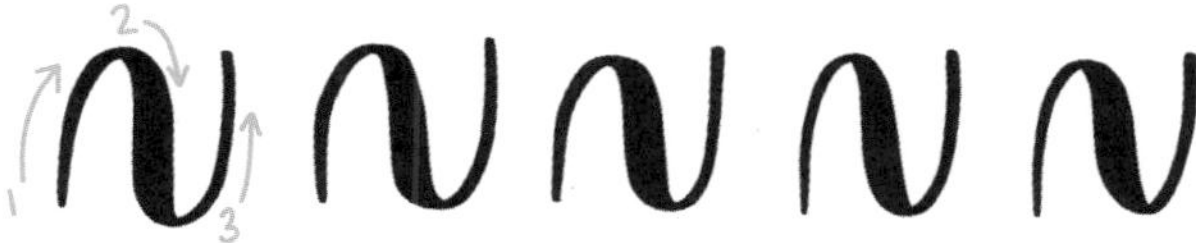

Use the space below to practice some of these compound curves. They may feel (and look) a little awkward at first, but, like everything, you'll find that they improve with practice. You can also try making several compound curves to form a longer squiggle before lifting your pen.

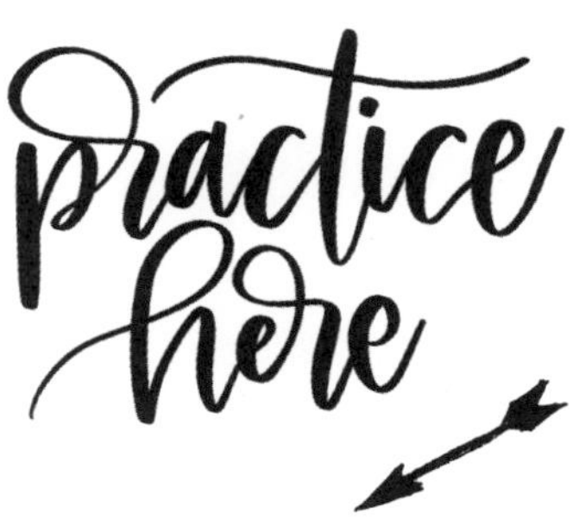

OVAL

The oval is a very useful shape for building commonly used letters like "a," "d," "g" and "o." Starting at the top, make a curving downstroke, then, at the bottom, switch to a curving upstroke that meets your starting point. I often think of it like an underturn that's closed at the top. Remember to gradually increase and decrease your pressure as you make the switch.

Practice some ovals in the space below.

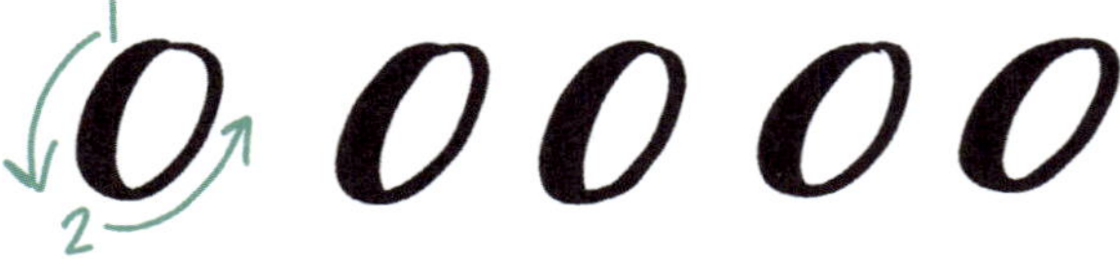

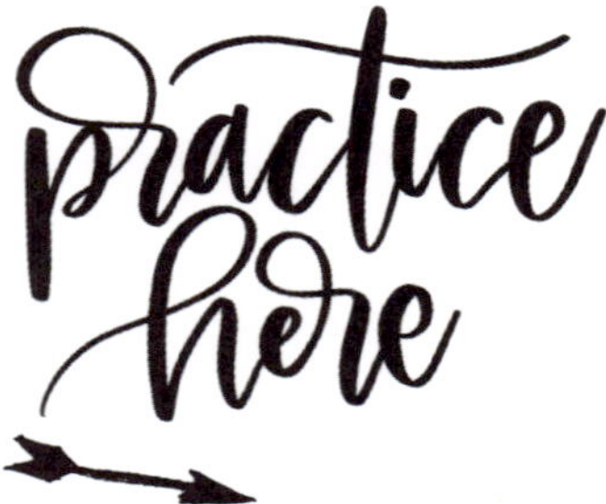

ASCENDER LOOP

This type of loop is much like an overturn, it just turns in the opposite direction! Start by drawing an upstroke, but when you get to the top, move your pen to the left instead of the right. Curve the line back down on itself, forming a loop, then let the line go straight down for your downstroke. We will go into more detail about ascenders and descenders in the chapter on flourishes (page 47).

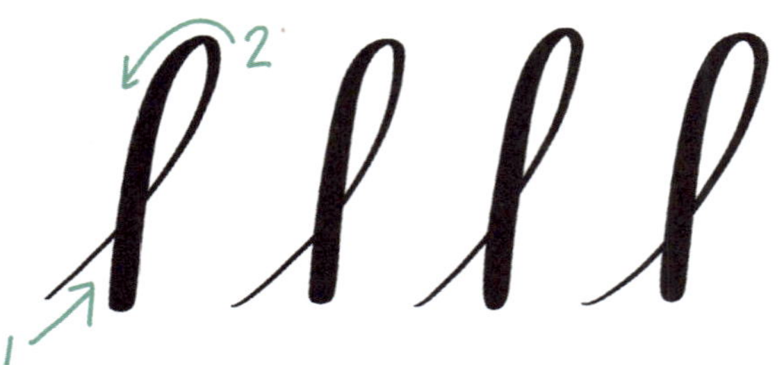

Letters like "b," "d," "h" and "k" use this ascender loop and, all by itself, this loop makes the lowercase letter "l." Use the space below to practice forming some loops. Try making them different sizes and widths for some extra variety.

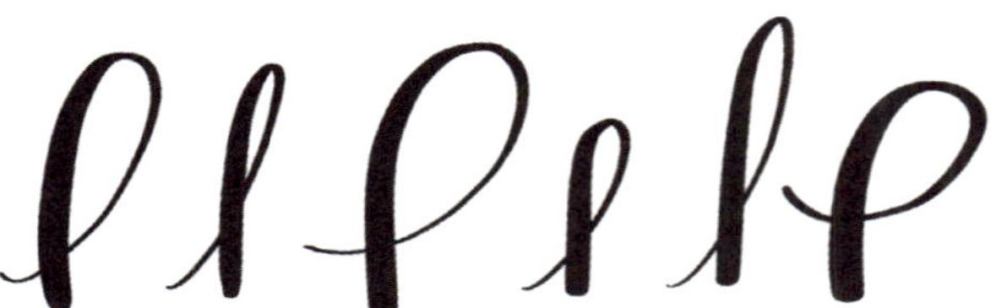

DESCENDER LOOP

Some letters have descender loops that go down below the rest of the word, like "g," "j," "p" and "y." This shape starts with a downstroke, then curves back up to the left like a backward underturn. Then, it continues to curve around to the right, crossing over the downstroke and forming a loop. As you practice this shape in the space below, you'll notice that if you add a dot on top, you're forming a lowercase "j."

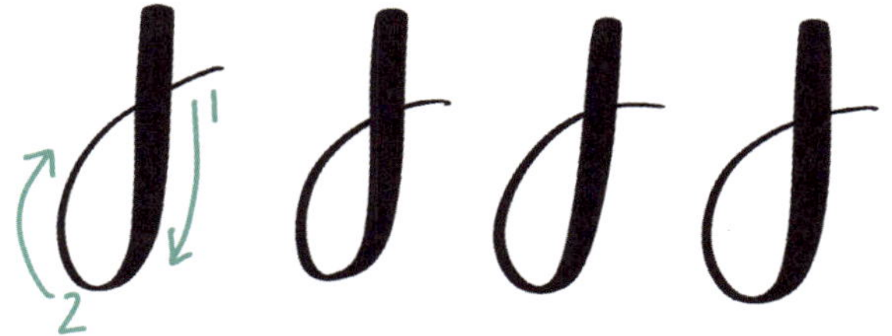

practice here

Way to go! You've officially learned the eight basic brushstrokes. Now, the key to mastering them is repetition. When I started lettering, I filled entire sketchbooks practicing these shapes. The next few tracing pages are designed to help you do some practice of your own. Feel free to look at my examples, trace over the provided strokes, then do some by yourself on the remainder of the lines. You can write directly on these pages right now or you can make copies of them first if you want some extra practice pages on hand. As we continue learning new skills, you may want to come back to practicing these drills from time to time, since they're the foundation of everything else.

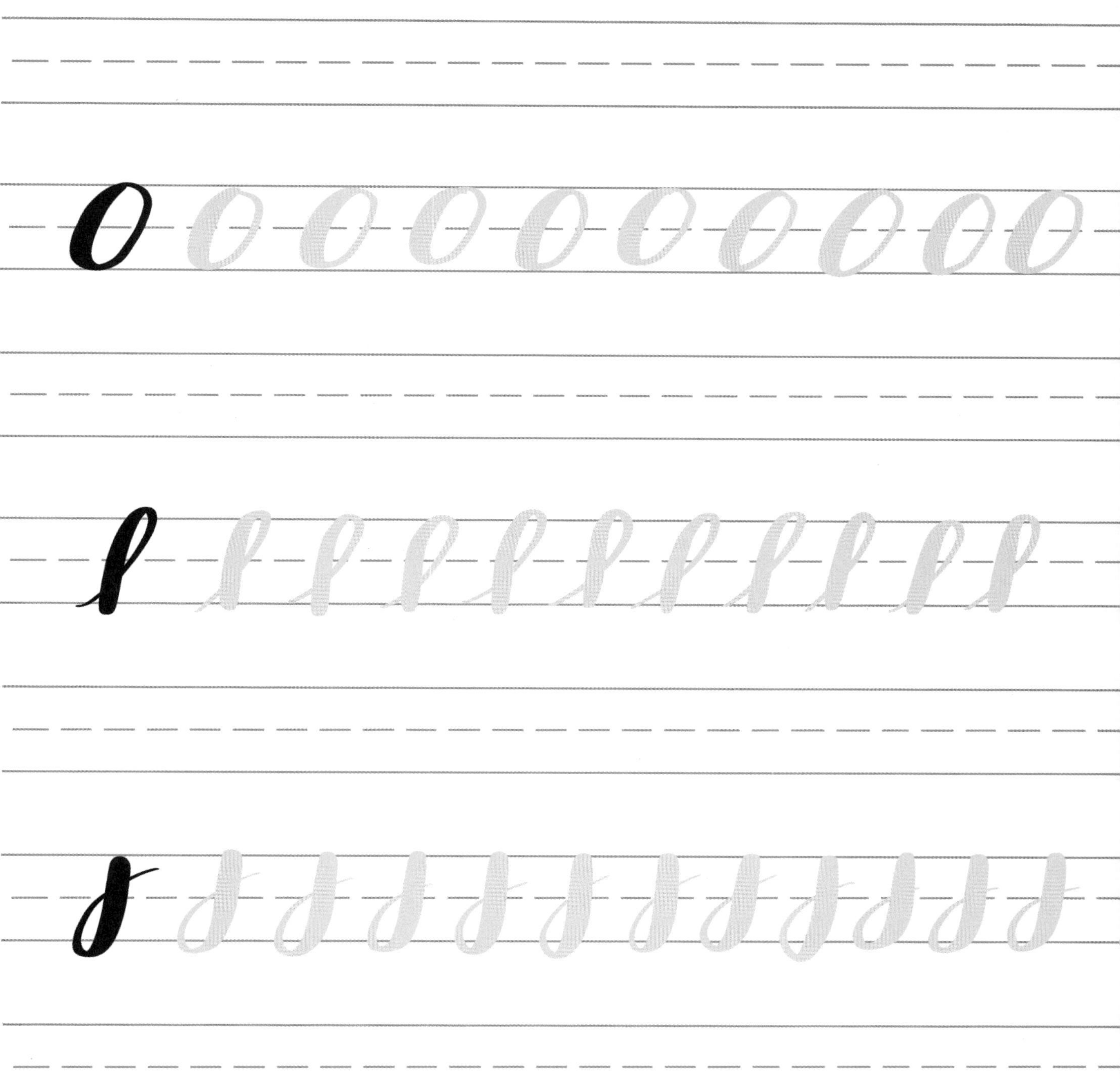

CHAPTER 3

The Brush Script Alphabet

The letters of the brush script alphabet are formed by combining the eight brushstrokes in different ways. Here are a few examples—take a look at these letters and try them with me.

a

A lowercase "a" is an oval plus an underturn. Remember that the underturn doesn't always go up to the full height of the letter; in this case, we want to stop it about halfway.

g

To form a "g," first make an oval, then add a descender loop on the right side.

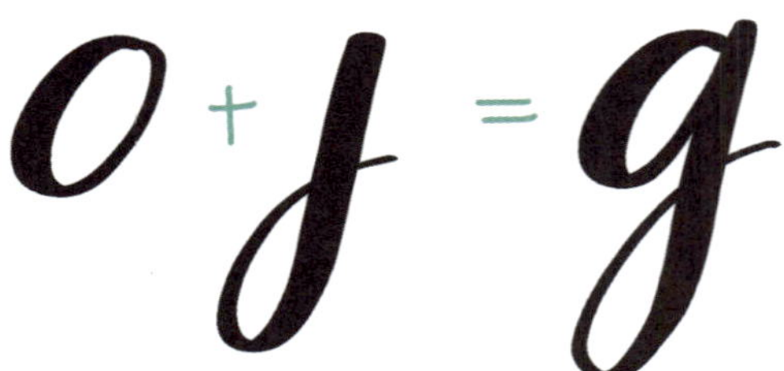

h

An "h" is just an ascender loop and a compound curve!

n/m

Draw a downstroke plus a compound curve to form the letter "n." Add a second compound curve and it becomes an "m"!

practice here

u

Our underturn, plus a second partial underturn, forms a "u." Make it a full second underturn and you have a "w."

y

An underturn with a descender loop on the right side is our letter "y."

As you work on each letter, feel free to pick up your pen in between the various strokes. Unlike cursive handwriting—where we are supposed to keep the pen on the paper at all times until the end of a word—hand lettering allows us to lift the pen anytime to achieve the look we want. Cursive writing sometimes involves retracing certain lines in a letter, but lettering does not. As you practice more, you can try flowing directly from one stroke into the next for some of your letters when it feels comfortable, but there's no rule saying you have to.

Are you ready to tackle the whole alphabet? The following pages are resources to help you do just that. I've given you a sample of each letter, along with a few examples to trace, then space to try it on your own. You can make copies of these pages for personal use if you want to have extras on hand for more practice.

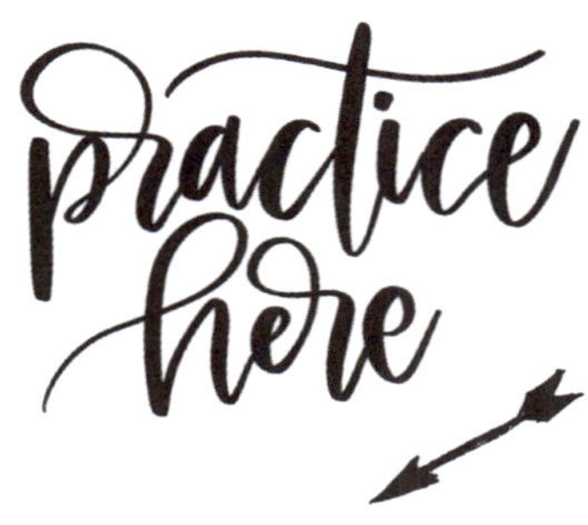

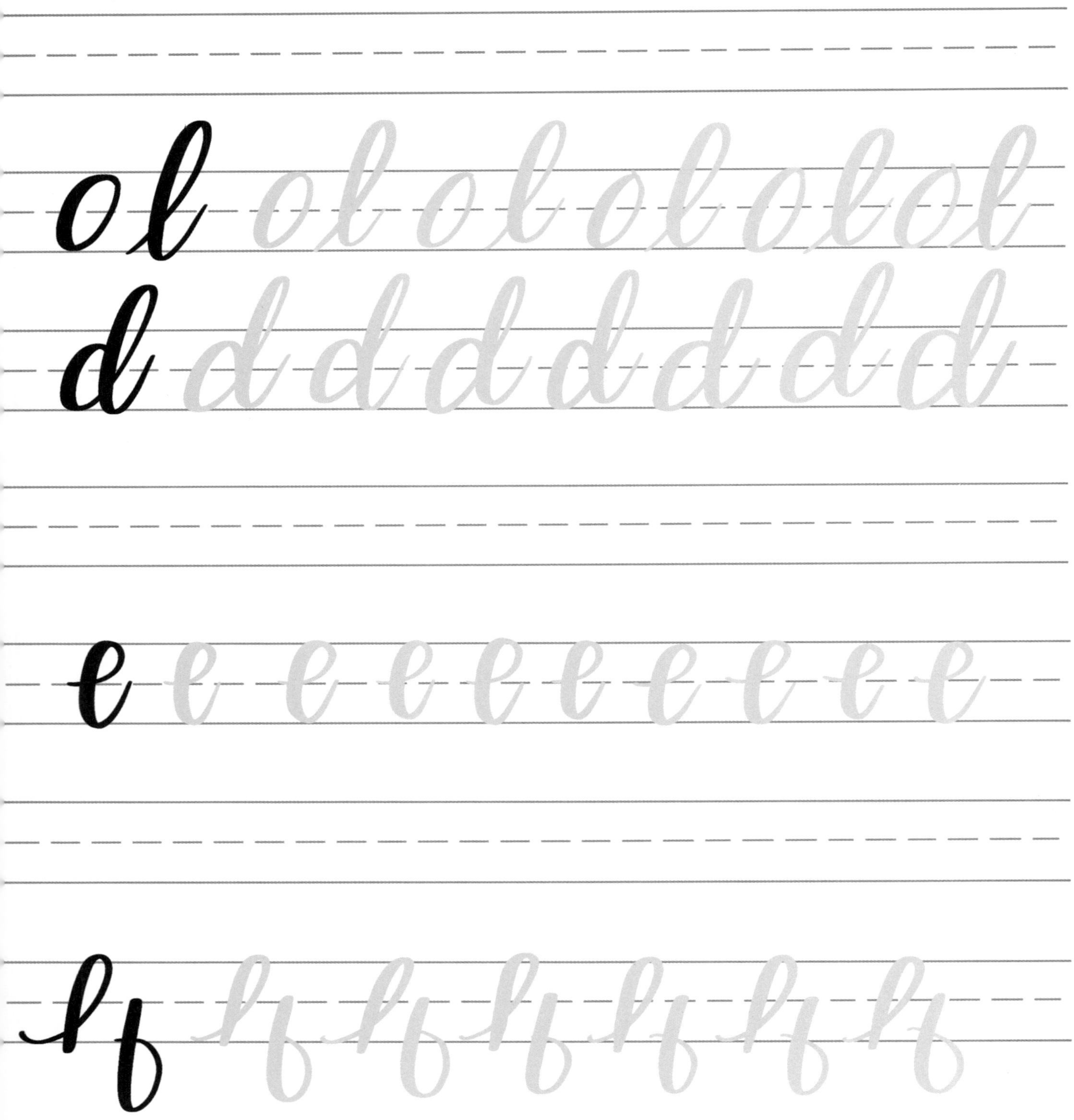

ol ol ol ol ol ol

d d d d d d d d

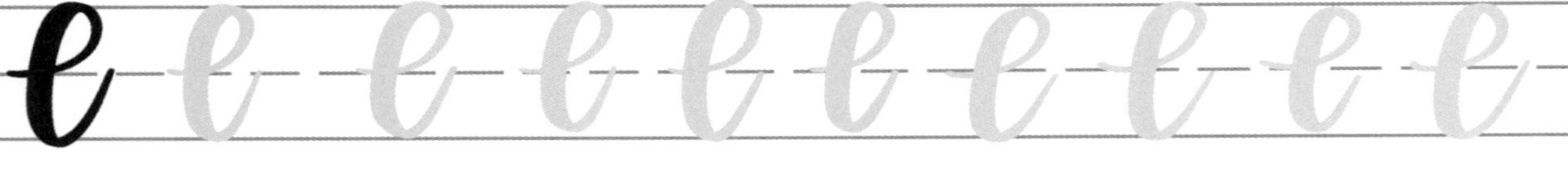

e e e e e e e e e e

f f f f f f f

i i i i i i i i i i i i i

j j j j j j j j j j j j j

k k k k k k k k

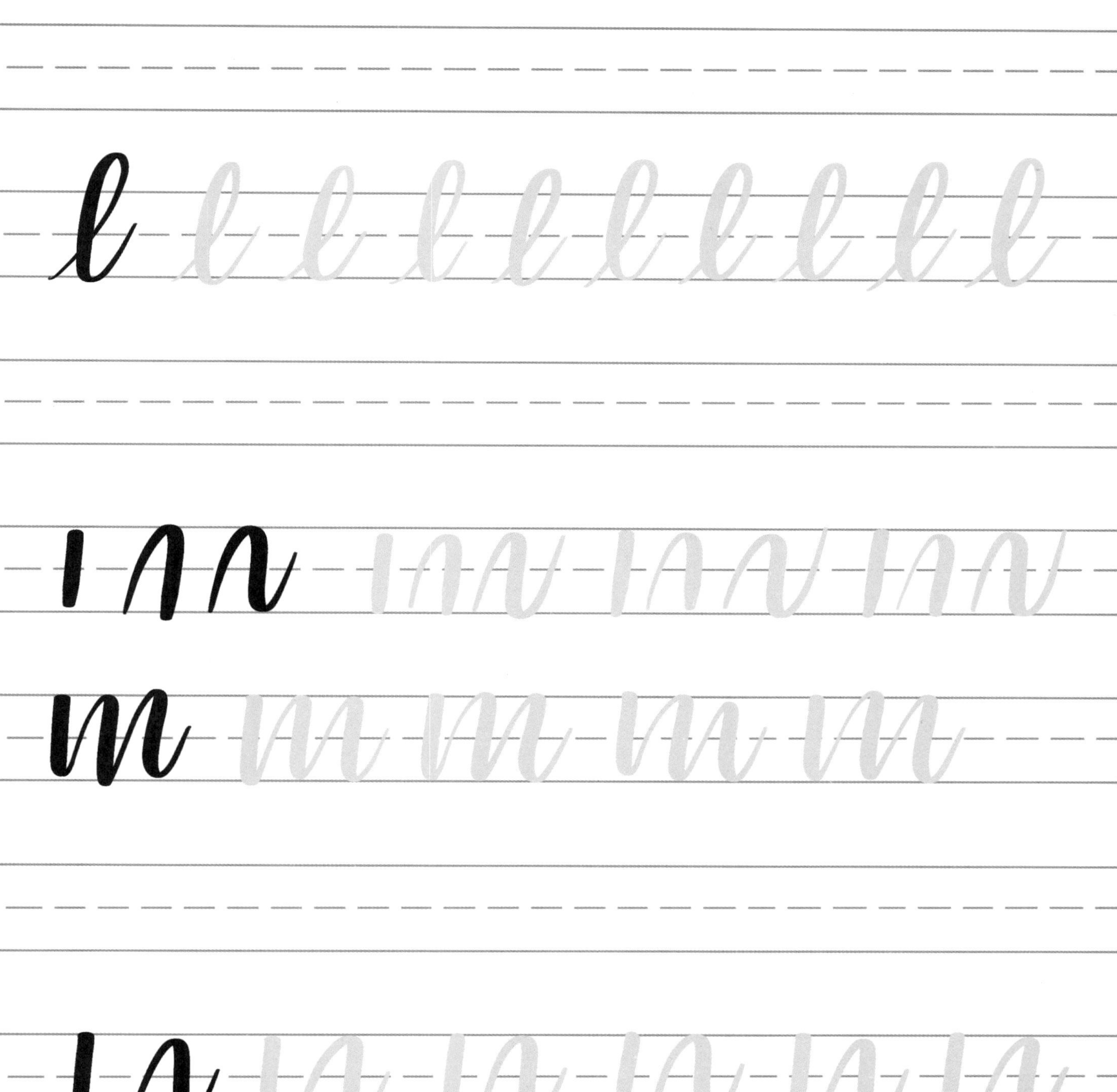

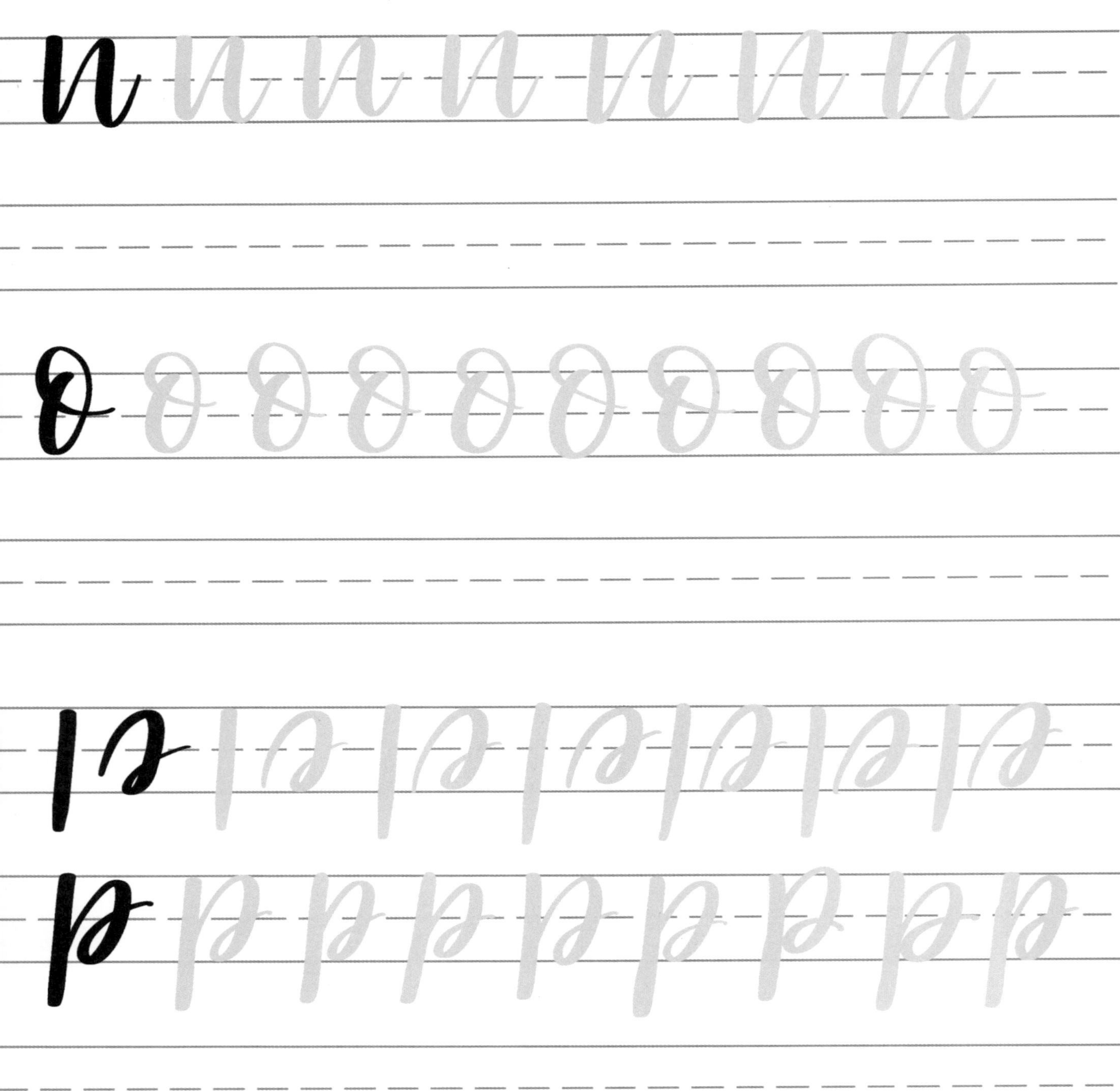

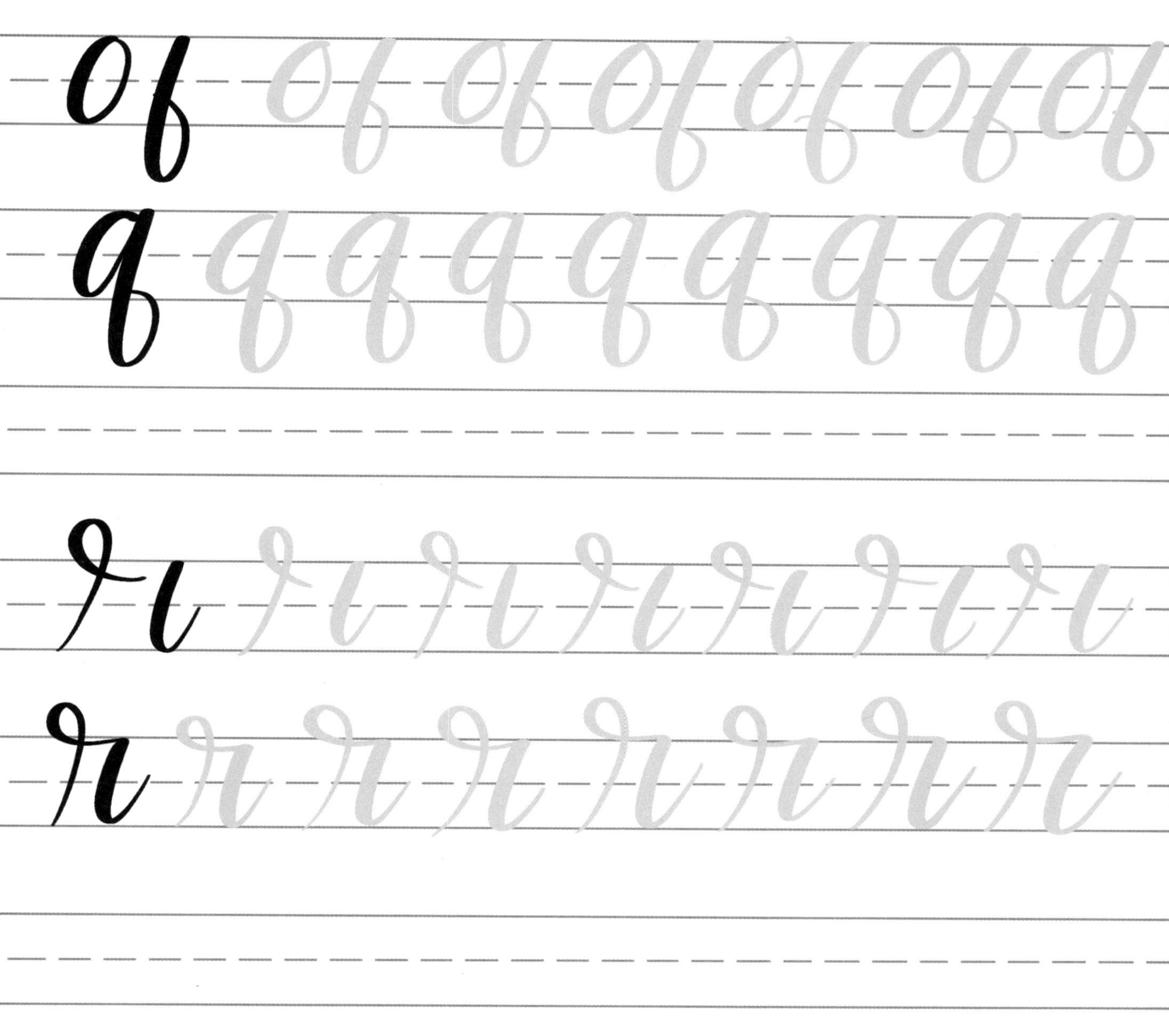

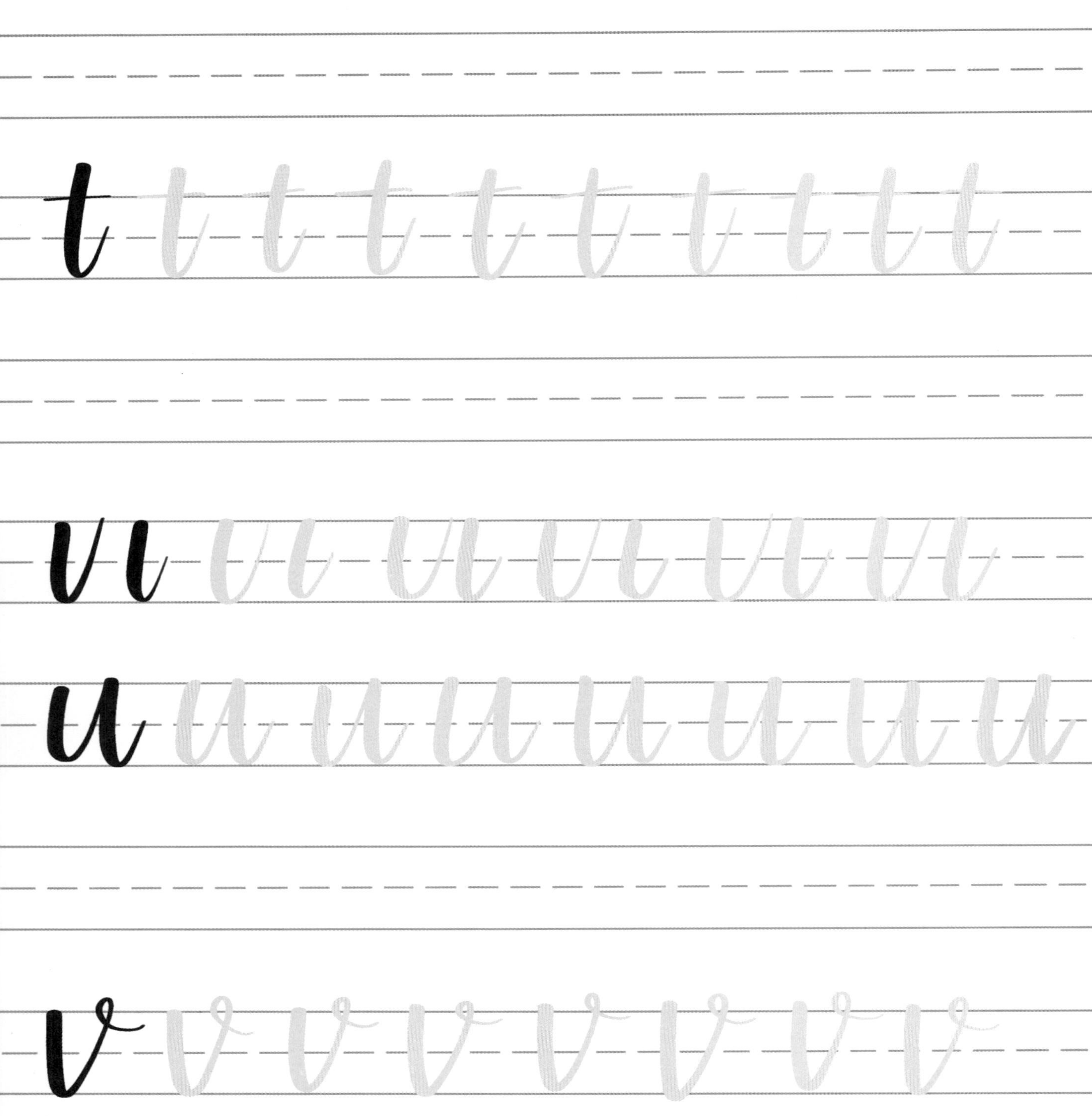

Y

y

Z

z

0123456789

0123456789

D

E

F

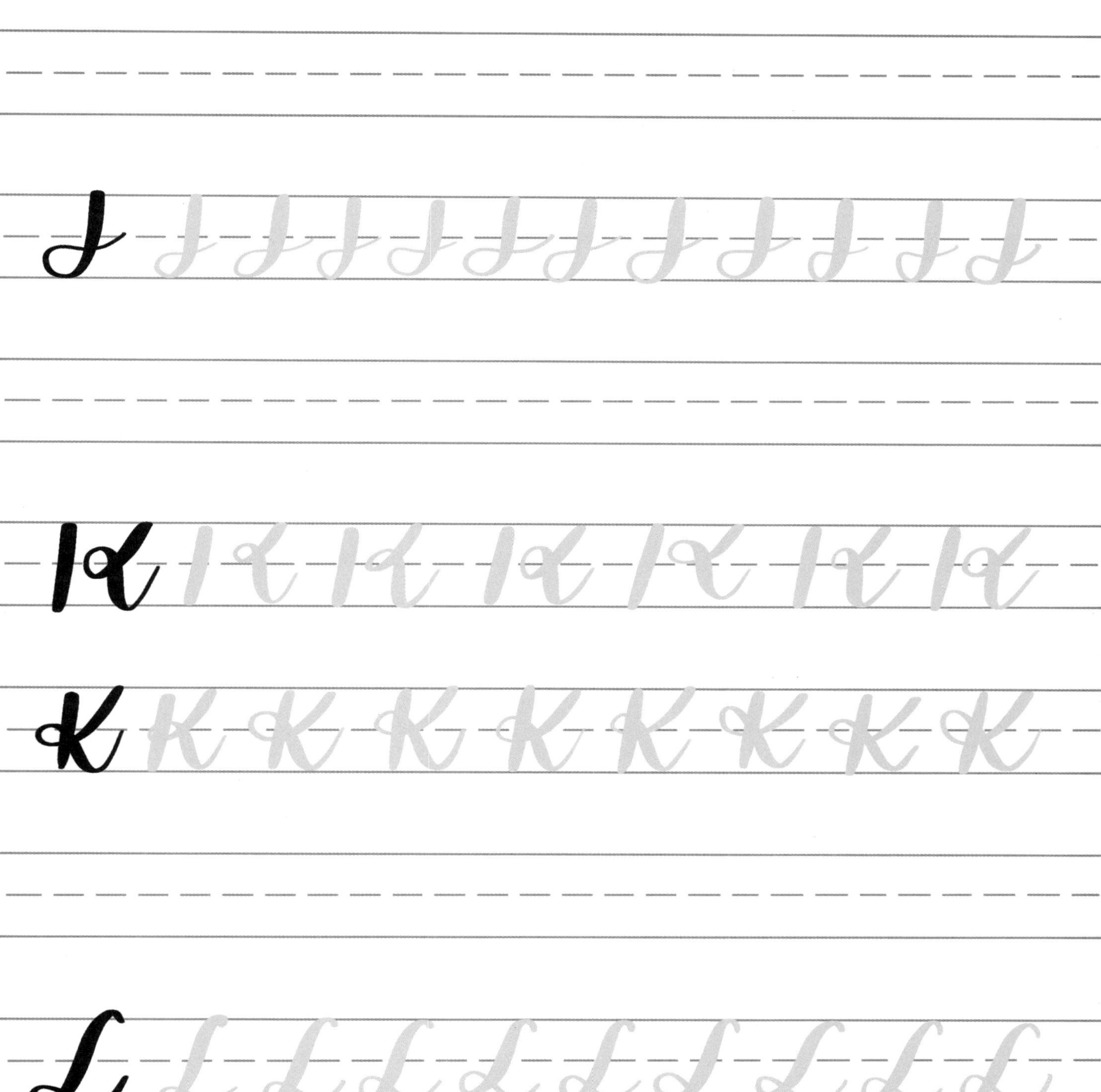

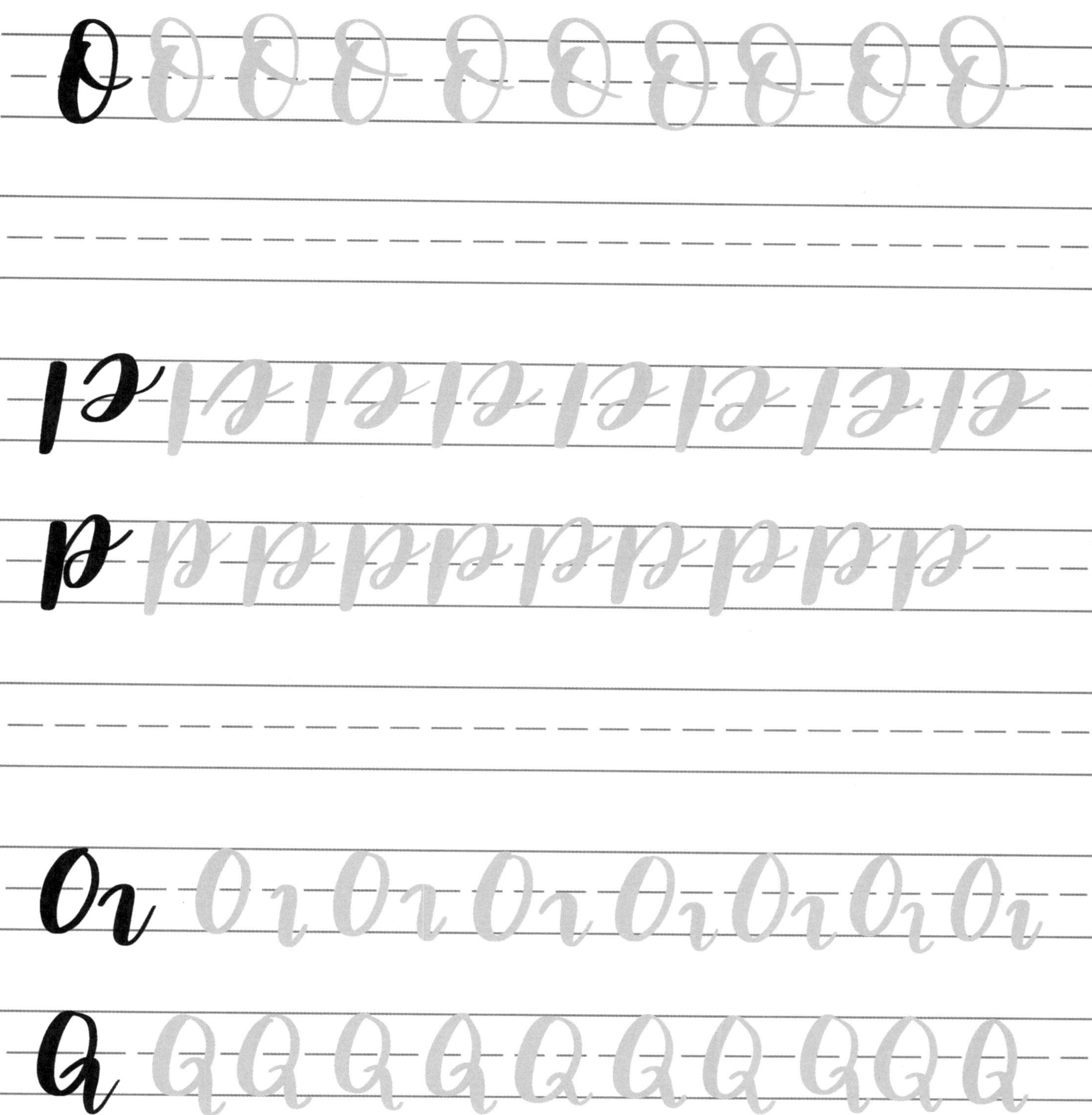

R

R

S

T

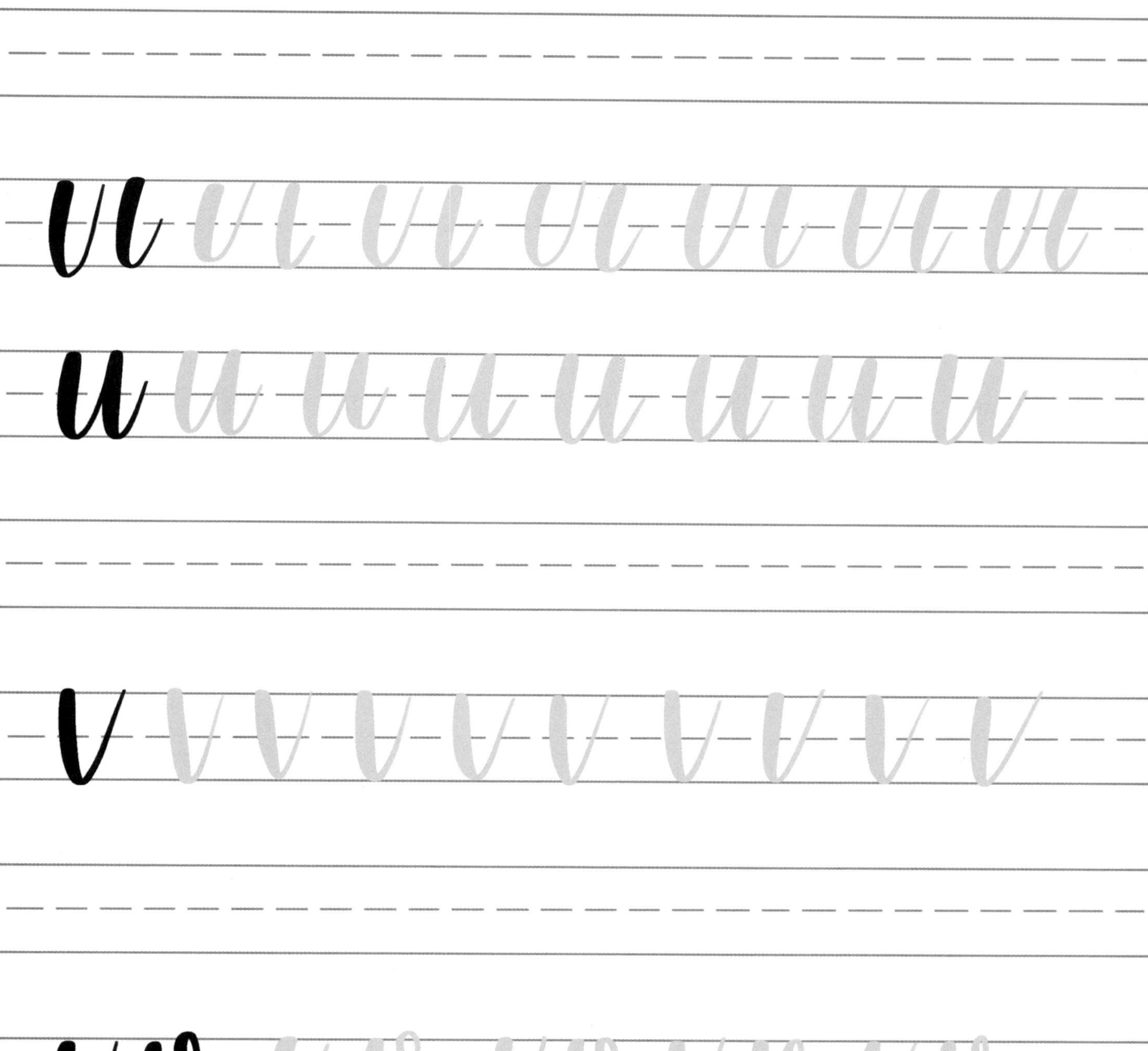

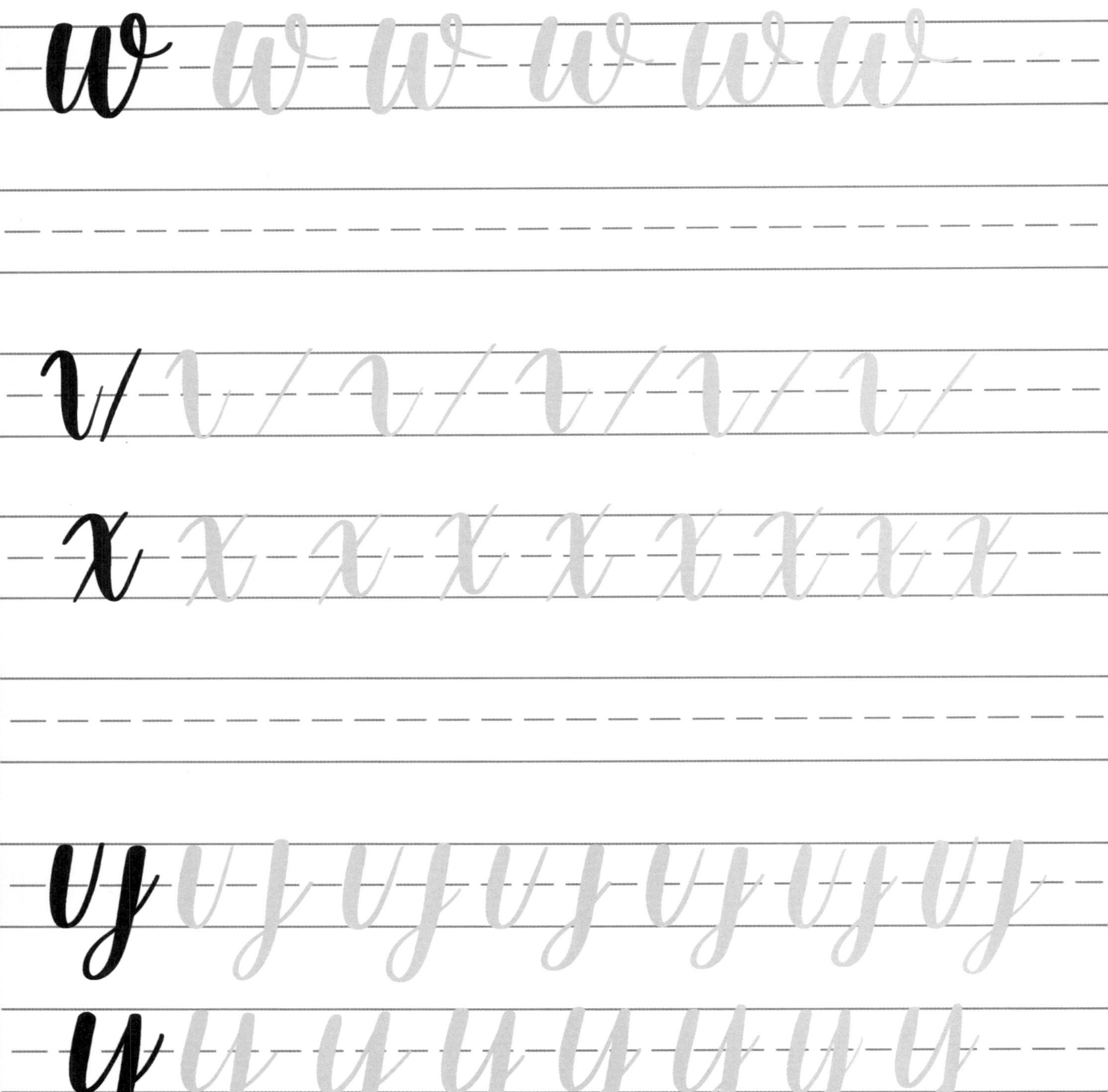

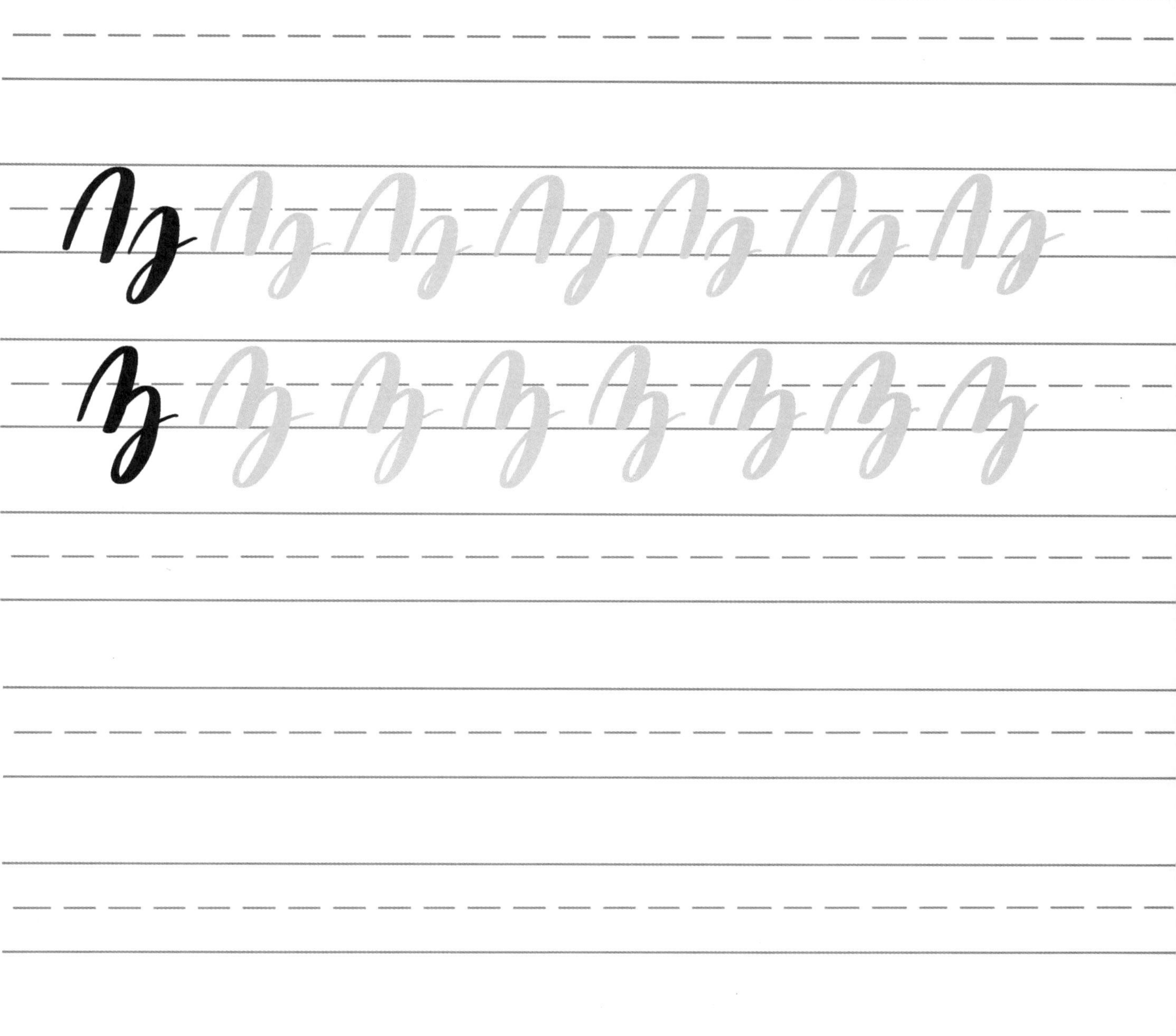

a b c d e f g h i j

k l m n o p q r s t

u v w x y z

A B C D E F G H I J

K L M N O P Q R S

T U V W X Y Z

0 1 2 3 4 5 6 7 8 9

CHAPTER 4

Brush Script Lettering

Now you know your abcs . . . with a brush pen! Creating a hand-lettered project is just one step away. All that's left to do is take these beautiful letters and connect them to each other to form words. As I mentioned in the previous chapter, this works a little differently in hand lettering than it does in cursive handwriting. When we write in cursive, there are places where, in order to connect our letters, we have to retrace a line we already wrote. Take a look at the example below of the word "mat."

In normal script writing, there are two places in this word where your pen goes back over a line you've already drawn. Write it for yourself on a piece of scrap paper or in the space below and you'll see what I mean. First, your pen goes up after the "m" to form the top of the "a," then retraces part of that line as the "a" loops around. Then, you form the tall line of the "t" and retrace it coming back down. The dashed lines below indicate the retraced spots.

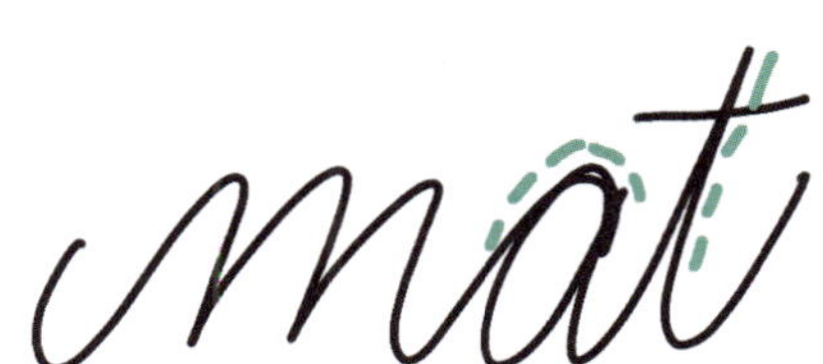

However, in brush script, we handle these areas differently. A basic rule of thumb you can follow is to lift your pen anytime you would have to retrace an existing line. Let's look at how this works using our sample word. When we write "mat" in brush script, first we'll write the "m," then pick up our pen before beginning the "a." We'll write the "a" and stop before beginning the downstroke of the "t." In the example below, I left a bit of space between the letters to show each separate pen movement, but, ideally, we want the letters to touch each other to give the appearance of being connected.

Here's how the word looks when everything is properly spaced.

In this particular example, following the rule meant lifting the pen at the end of each letter; however, that won't always be the case for every word. For example, when writing the word "love" in cursive, the only retracing we do is at the top of the letter "o."

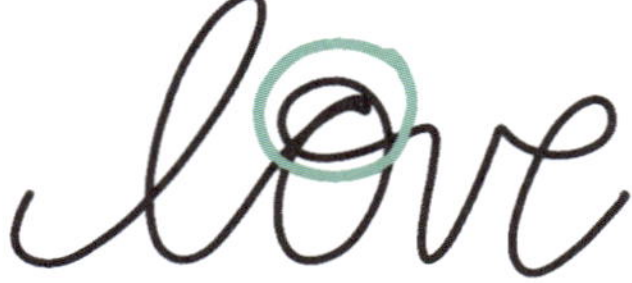

That means we pick up the pen after the first letter, "l," but we can easily connect the remaining three letters together without having to retrace any of our lines. Take a look:

This time, we only have to lift our pen twice: once after the first letter, then again at the end of the word.

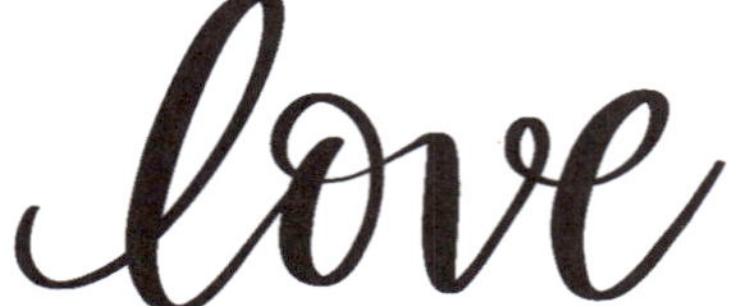

Here are a few more sample words broken down into pen strokes to help you get a feel for following this pattern. On the left, you'll see each lift of the pen indicated by a dot. Notice that each word is different based on which letters are next to each other. Over time, you'll begin to have a feel for where the pen needs to lift in order to avoid retracing your lines.

s·m·ile smile

wor·d·s words

ar·t art

he·ar·t heart

le·t·t·er letter

h·a·n·d hand

wr·i·te write

You'll start to know what feels natural and do it without even thinking. In the meantime, feel free to use these practice words as you get the hang of things. Remember, it's not a matter of "right" or "wrong," just a general guideline that should help make your lettering look and feel cohesive.

Take some time to practice writing a few words in the provided practice space. You can try the ones illustrated above or any other words that are meaningful to you. It may feel strange at first to lift the pen mid-word, but I promise it will become part of your muscle memory just like the rest of the brush technique.

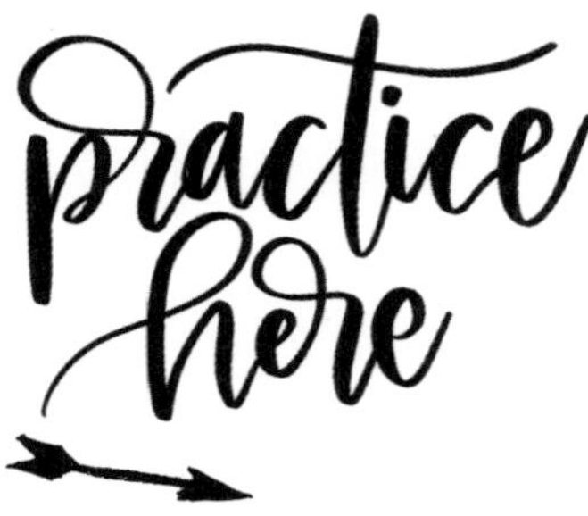

CHAPTER 5

Flourishes

Once you've gotten the hang of the basic alphabet, adding flourishes is a great way to elevate your brush lettering. There are several parts of letters that lend themselves perfectly to being embellished: ascenders, descenders and crossbars. So, what in the world are they? An ascender is a line that goes up higher than the rest of the letter and the neighboring letters. A descender is a line that extends down below the letter's baseline. A crossbar is when you use a horizontal line to intersect part of a letter, like when you cross a "t" or draw a horizontal line through the capital "A" or "H."

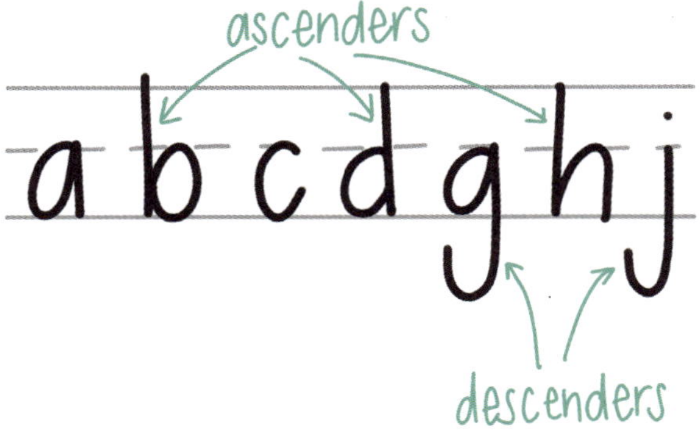

ASCENDER FLOURISHES

First, let's take a look at some easy ascender flourishes. These can be used for letters that have an ascender, like "b," "d," "h" or "k." Here are a few of my favorite ways to make those ascenders look extra special. One is simply to make the ascender into an extra-large loop. Another is to begin the loop with a counterclockwise swirl, or you can begin the loop with a flourish that resembles the number "2."

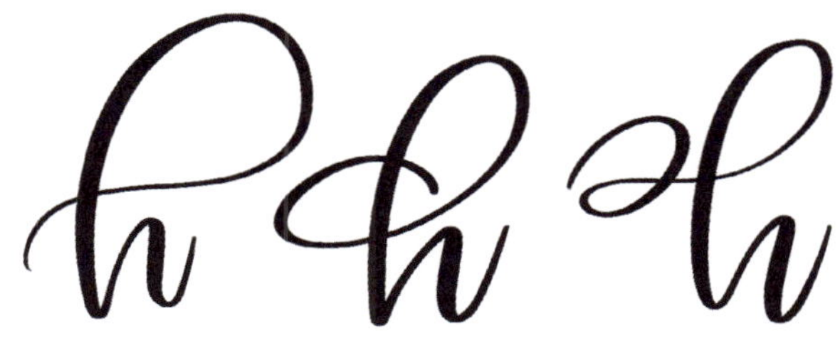

Now, it's your turn! Let's practice those ascender flourishes, keeping in mind that, just like in the rest of our lettering, anytime your pen is moving downward, you'll want to apply more pressure. As always, downstrokes are the thickest part of our letters, even the swirly flourished ones.

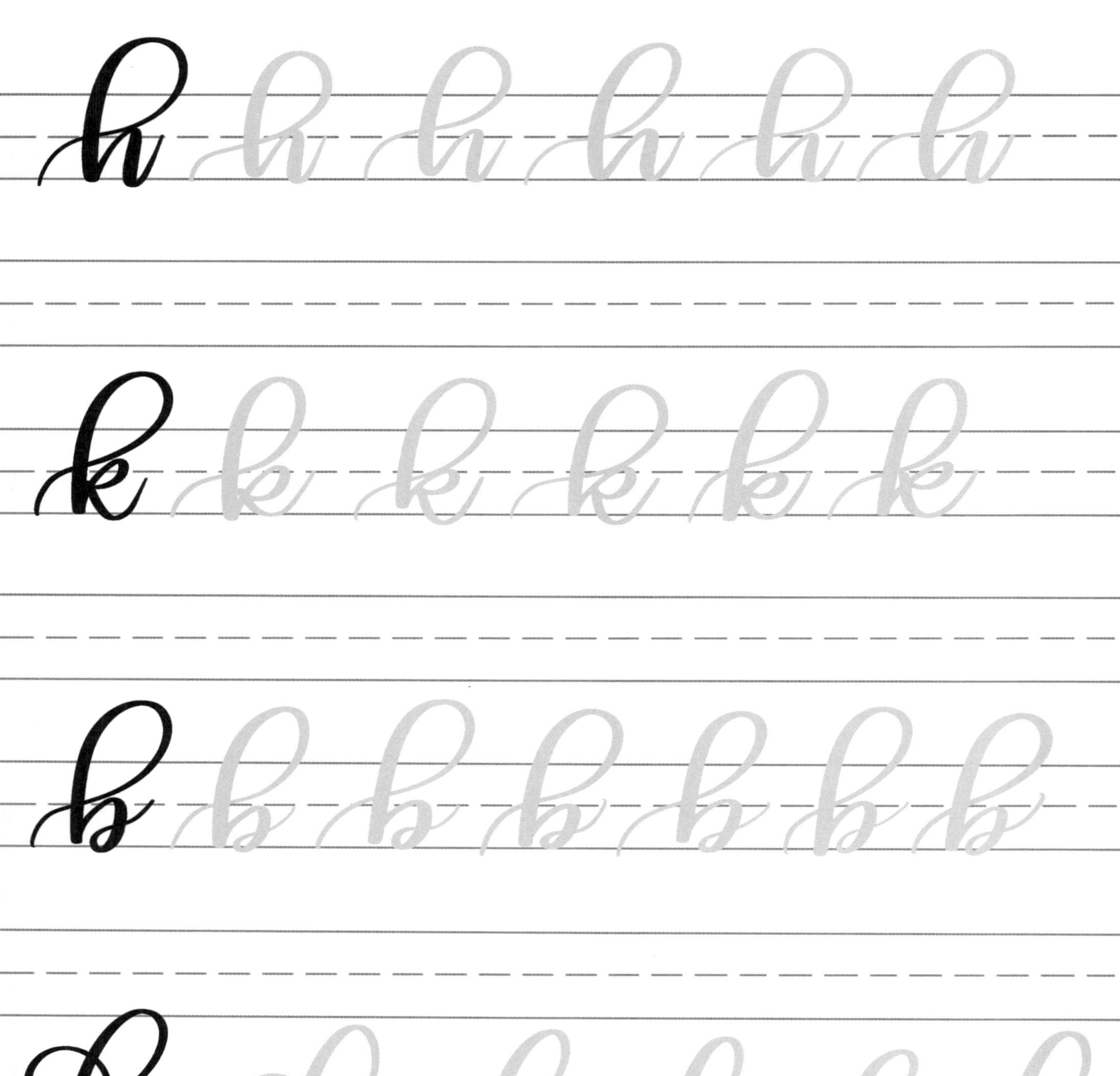

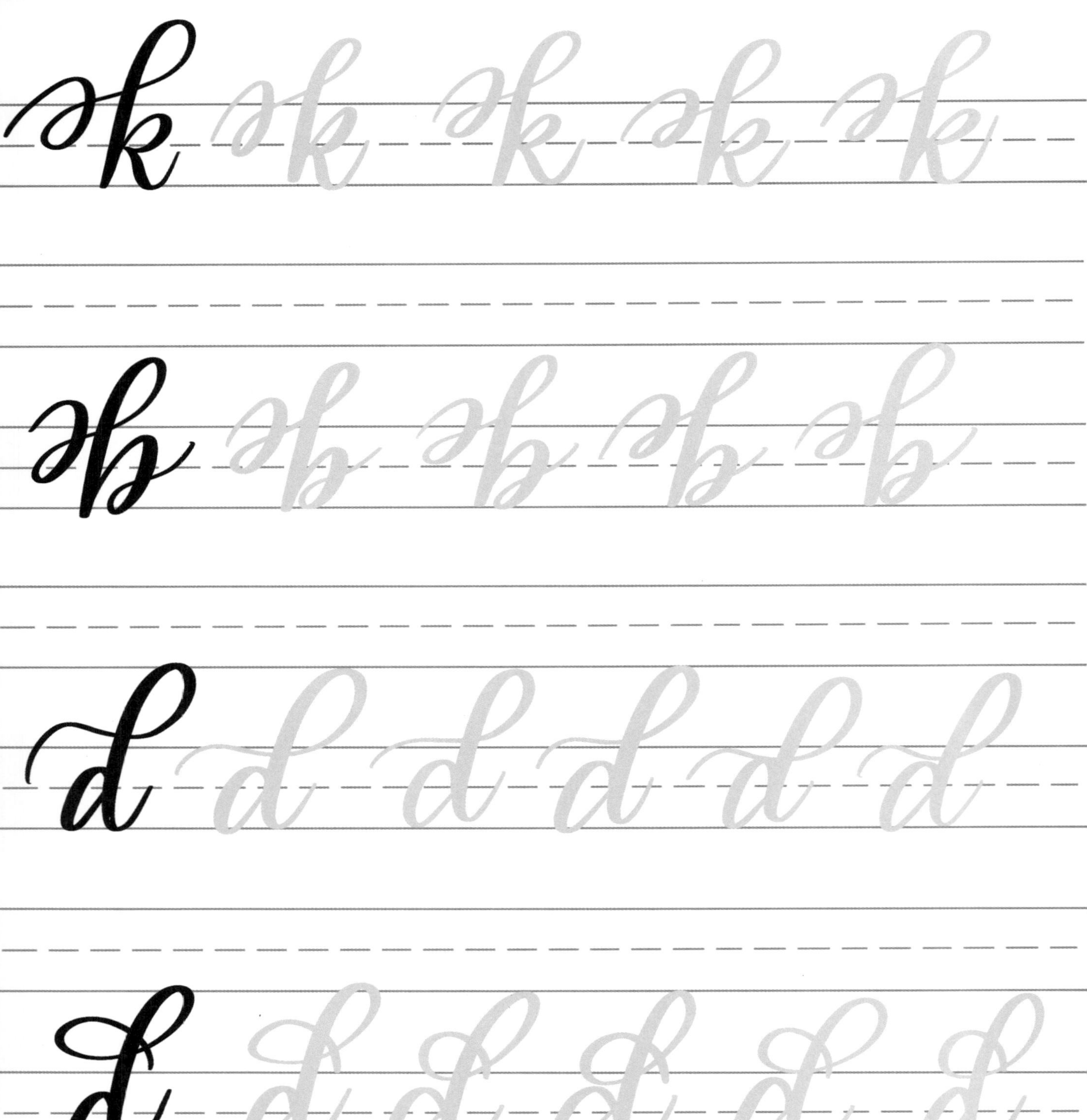

DESCENDER FLOURISHES

Now, let's take a look at how we can flourish our descenders; for example, in the letters "y," "j" and "g." Here are a few fun and fancy ways to jazz them up. First, we can continue our loop around into a curling line that crosses back over the descender itself. Another option is to add a smaller loop inside the large one, or to make that small loop, then continue out to the left. Finally, we can create that small loop, then cross our line back through it and out the other side of the letter.

Take some time to practice these embellishments by tracing mine, then try them on your own. Feel free to experiment, too, and play around with your own ideas for flourishing!

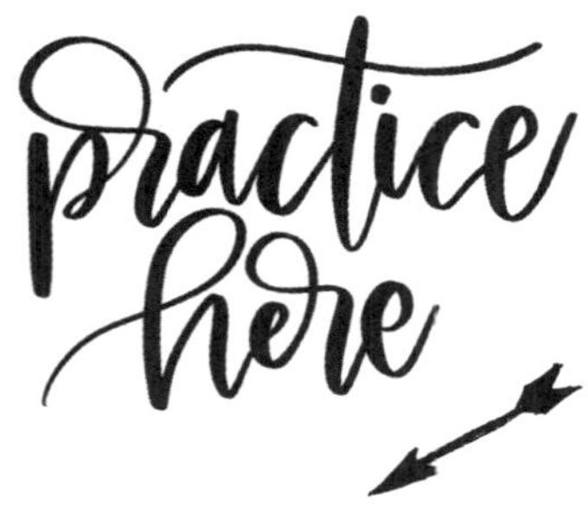

g g g g g g g g g

y y y y y y y y

j j j j j j j

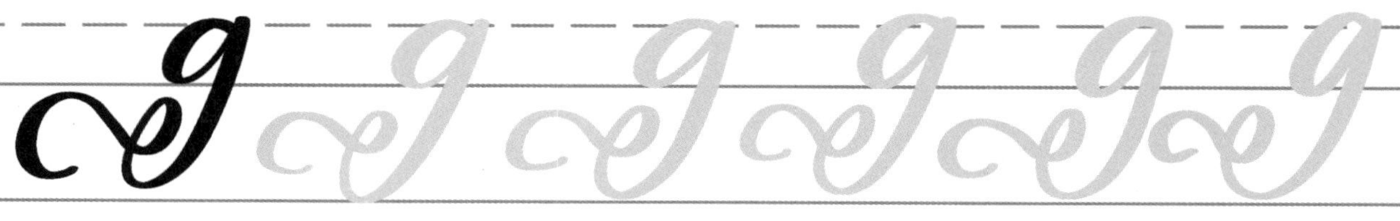

CROSSBAR FLOURISHES

The letter "t" gives us a unique opportunity to add a flourish every time we write it by playing around with the crossbar. We can extend it on one or both sides, curl it, swirl it and use it to fill in empty space. Take a look at a few of my favorite methods for crossing a "t."

Now, use the practice pages to try these different variations yourself! As you begin creating projects, you'll find that the letter "t" appears fairly often and you'll have lots of opportunities to make it look fabulous with your favorite form of embellishment.

These aren't the only flourishes you can add to your brush script—there are tons of other ways to embellish parts of letters and even combine pieces of letters together. As you continue to learn and create, you'll expand your repertoire. I like to think of learning lettering like having a toolbox that you continue to fill with more and more options as you learn new techniques. Then, when it's time to create something, you can open up that toolbox and choose what you want to use for that particular project.

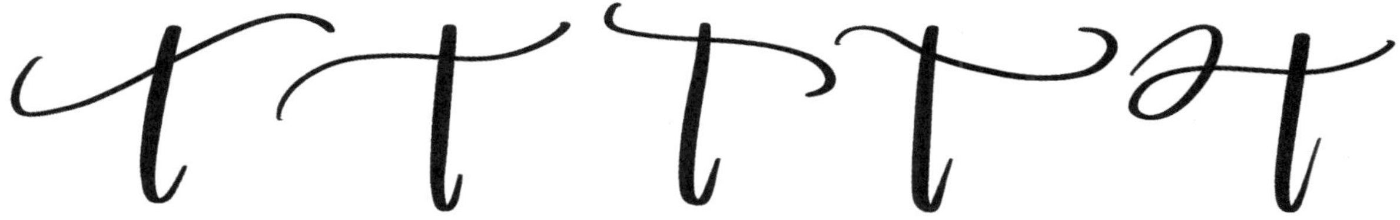

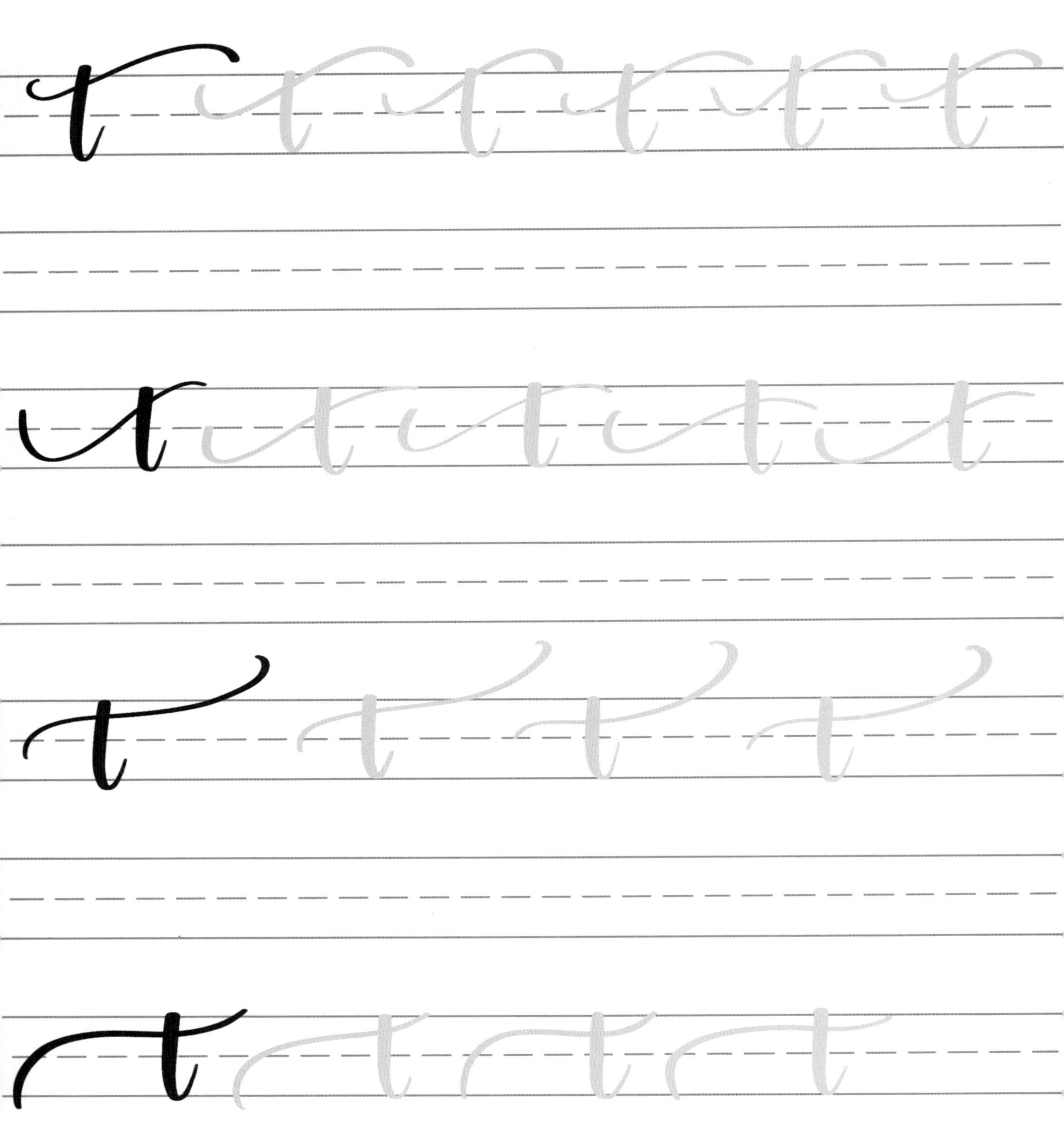

at

er

th

CHAPTER 6

Extended Brush Script

Once you've learned how to connect your script letters, there are lots of variations you can try that will give your brush lettering the look of an entirely different font. For example, simply by increasing the amount of space between a letter and the one that follows it, you'll create an elegant, elongated effect. Take a look at the word below, written with normal spacing, then written in this extended style. The brushstrokes are still the same; we form the letters the same way and lift our pen following the same rules, but we space the letters farther apart. While any brush pen can create this style, I personally prefer the look of a pen with a small tip, like the Tombow Fudenosuke. I recommend using a Fudenosuke—or something of a similar brush size—for completing the exercises in this chapter.

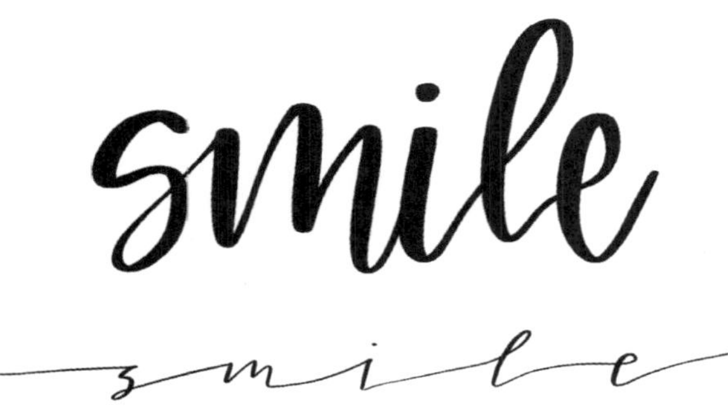

To try this variation, let's start with some practice forming each letter with a long horizontal line before and after it to create that extra space. Remember, horizontal lines are not downstrokes, so we don't apply much pressure, and those lines should remain light and thin. On the next page you can see the whole alphabet written in this style. I've only included the lowercase alphabet letters, because I find that using capitals in this style throws off the visual balance of the effect. If you'd like to use capitals, though, you can certainly give it a try in your own practice and projects!

Now, it's your turn. Use the practice pages provided to trace, then create your own elongated brush letters. Don't forget to always apply pressure when you get to a downstroke! The technique and the basic letter formations are still the same.

a b c

d e f

g h i

j k l

m n o

p q r

s t u

v w x

y z

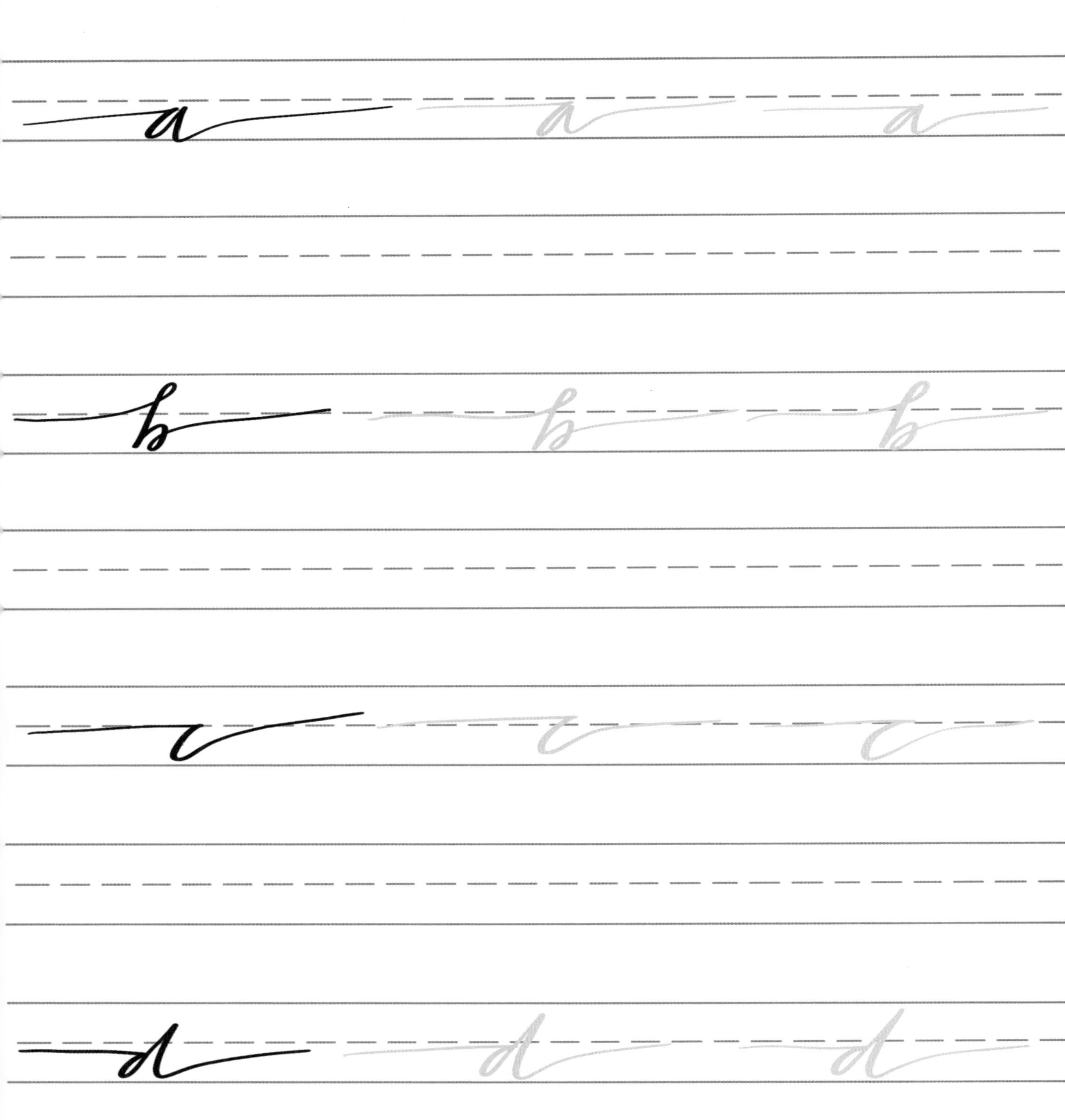

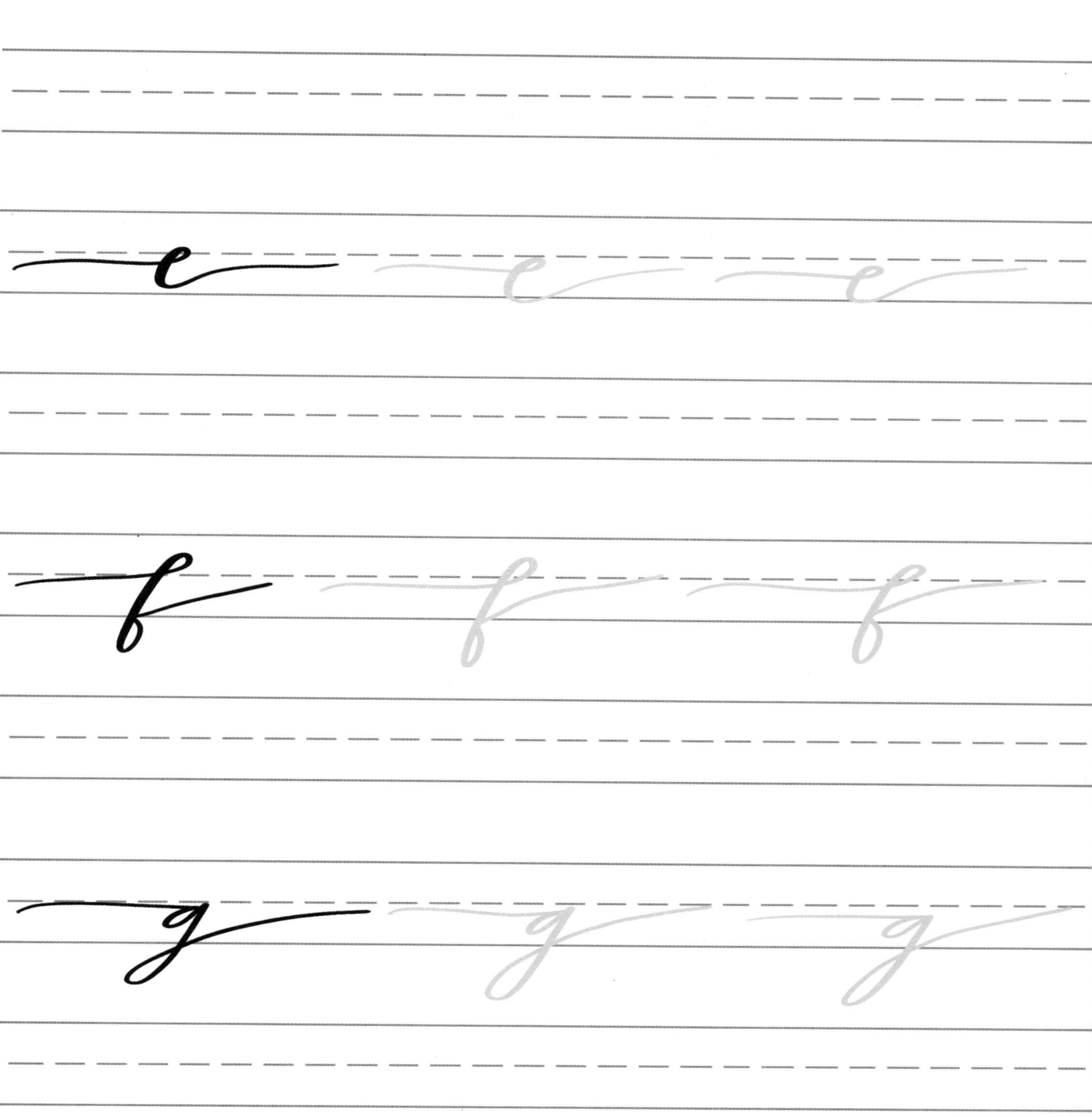

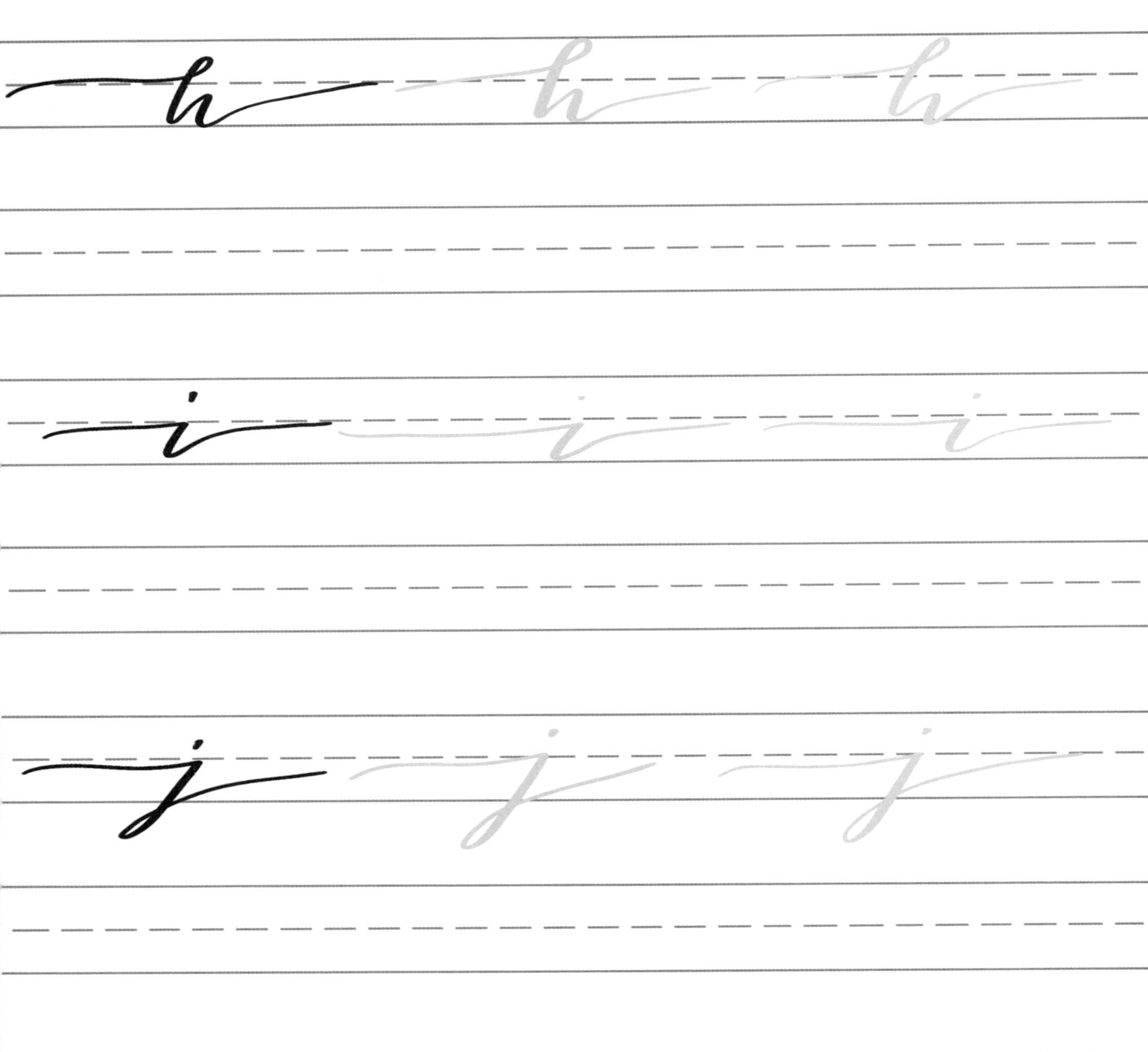

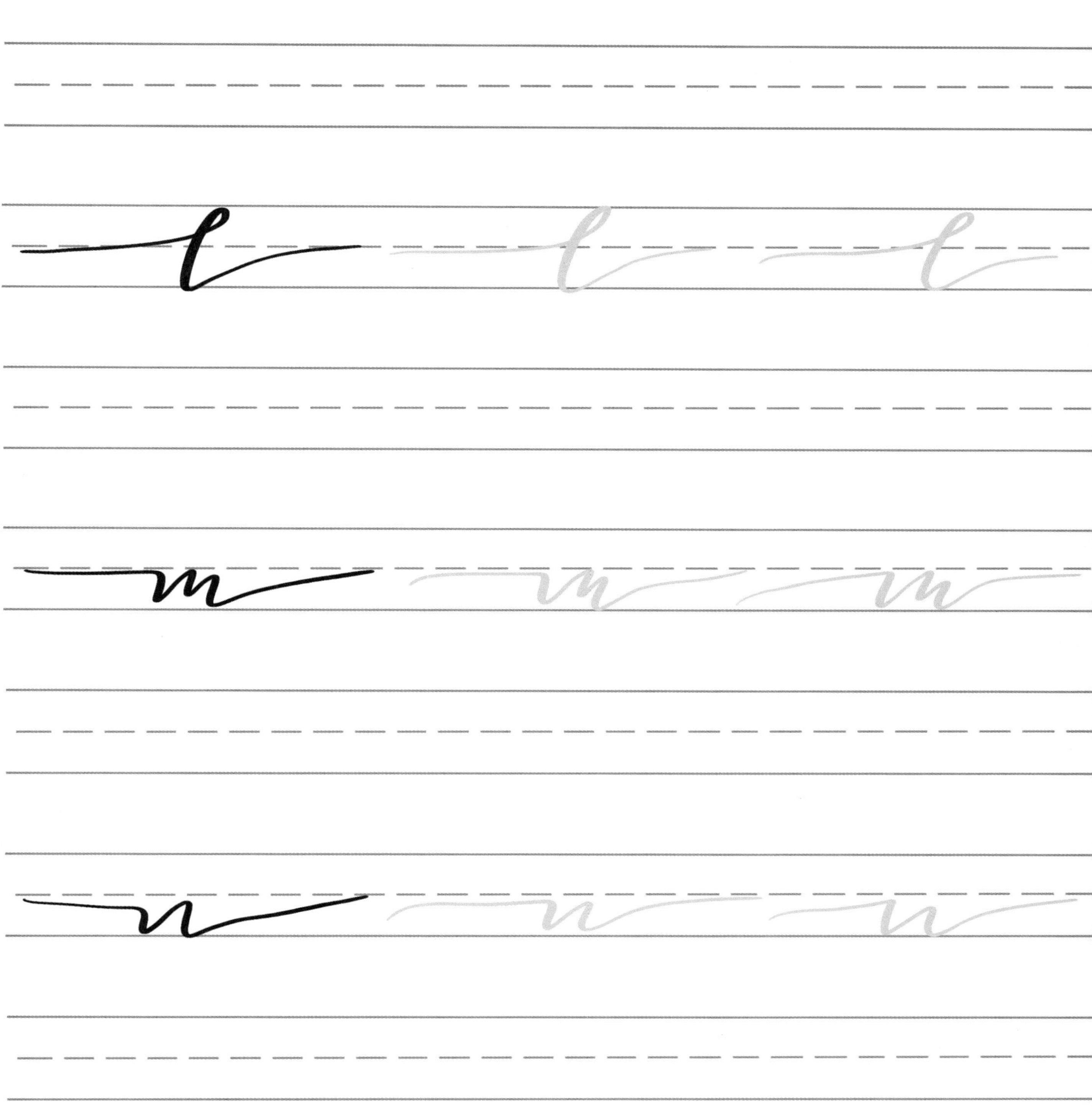

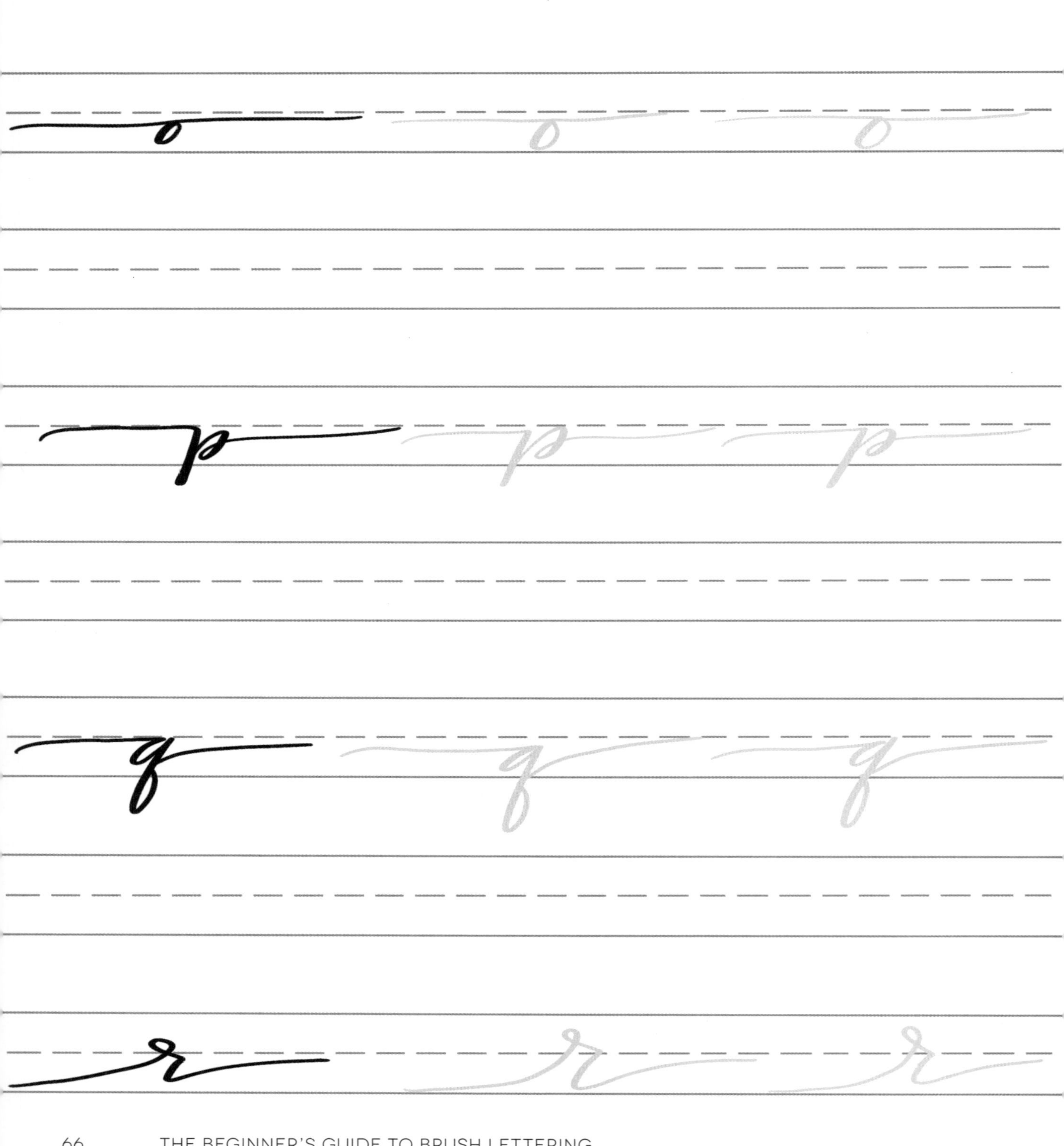

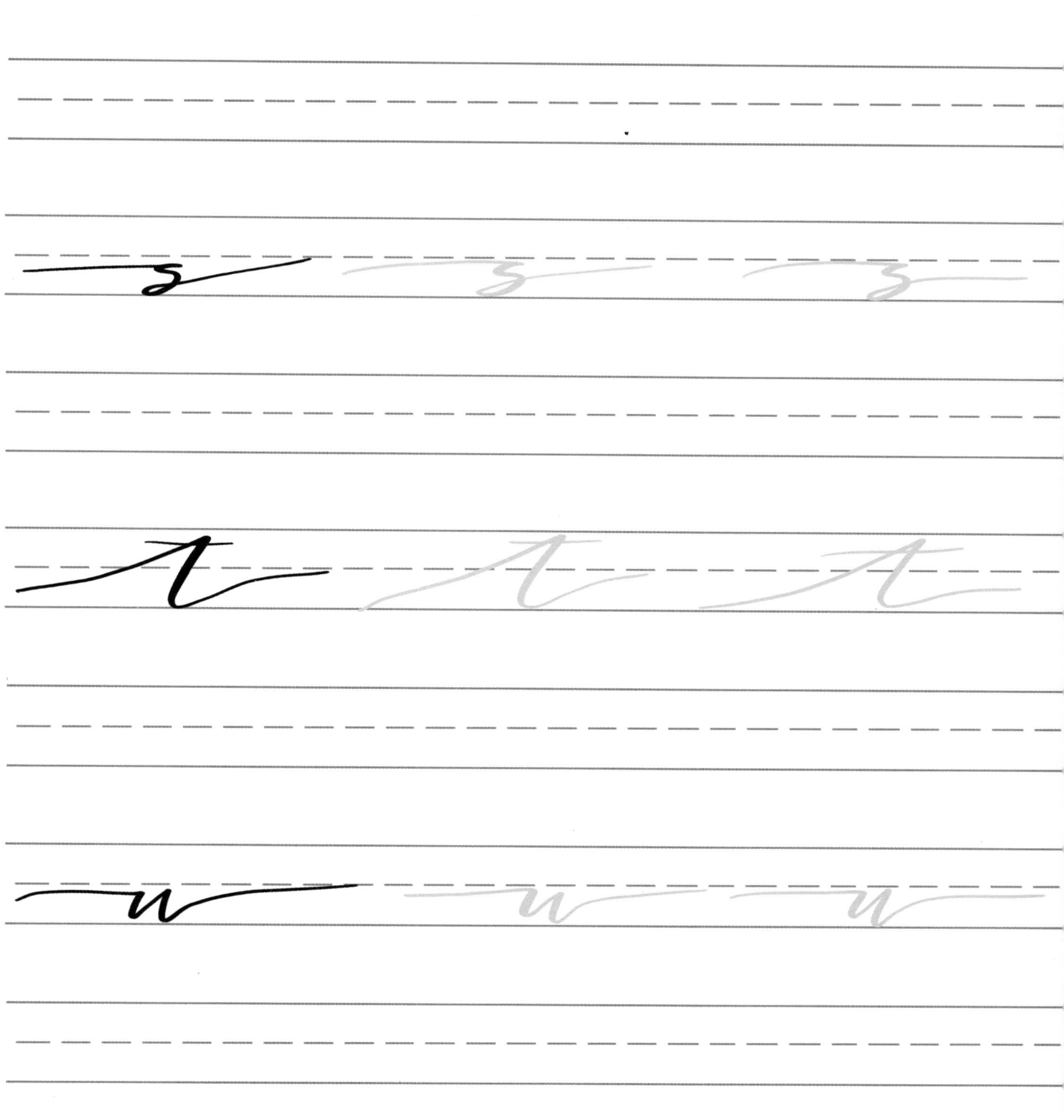

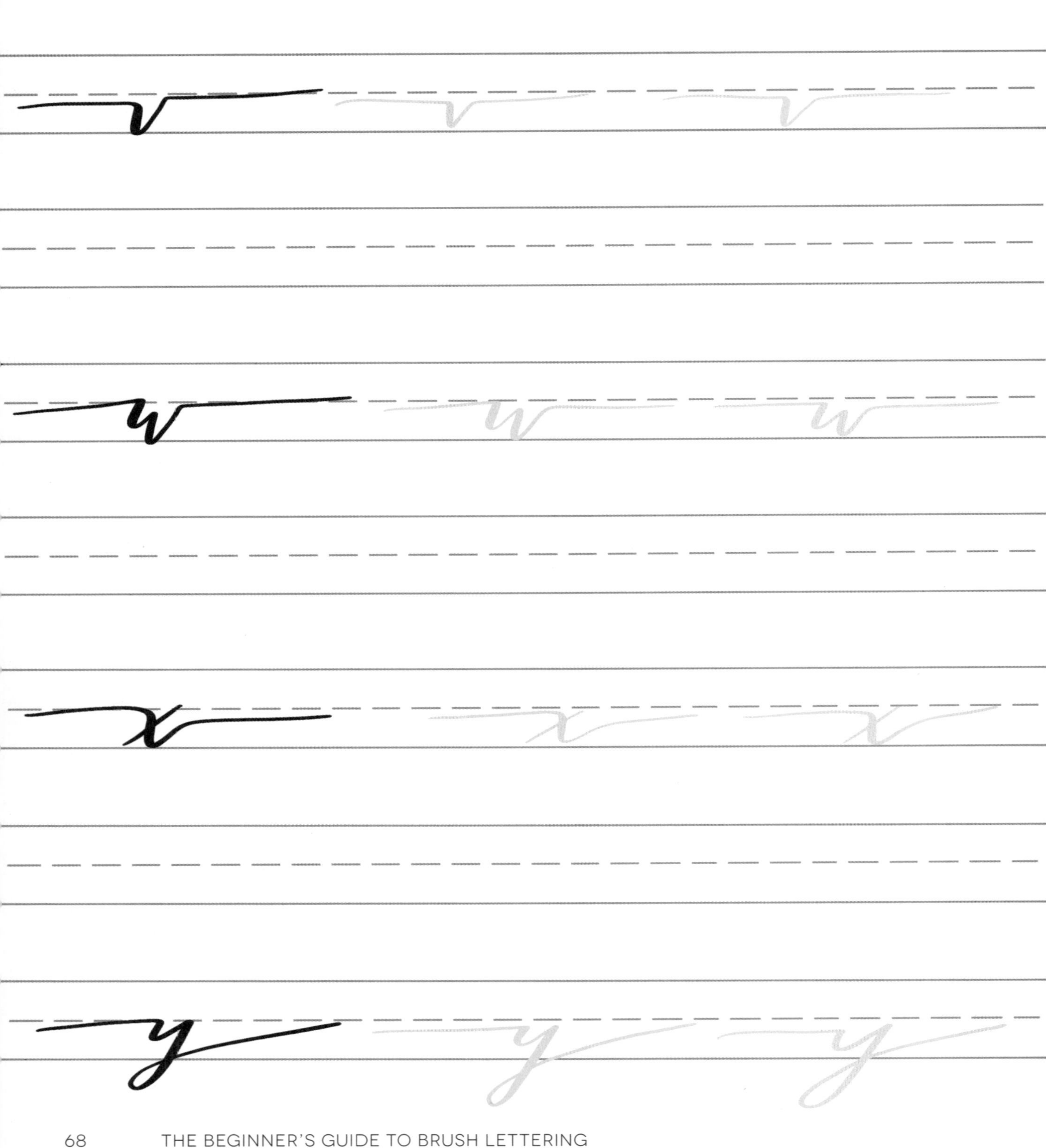

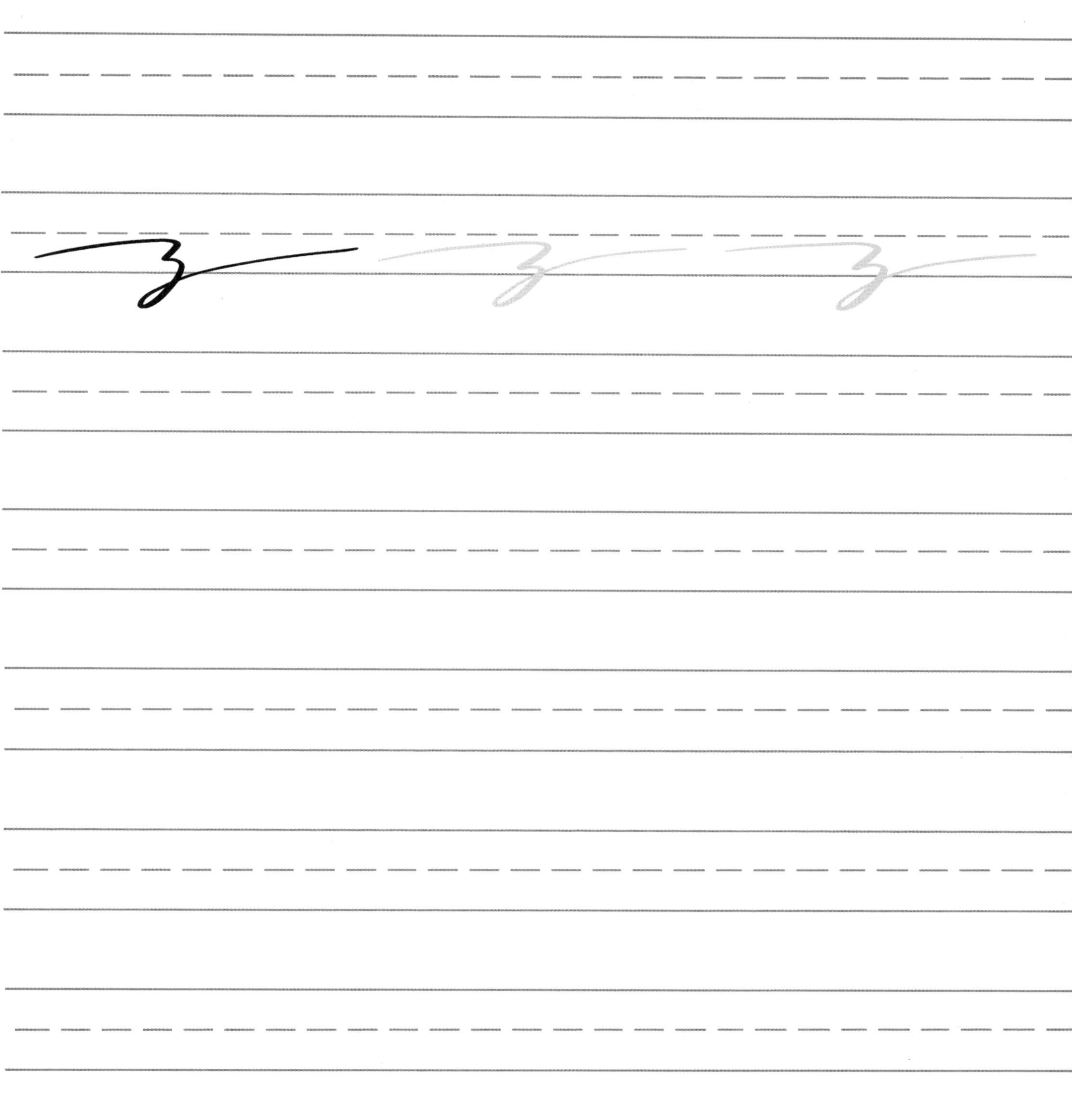

After all that practice, it's time to put our letters together to form a few words. Let's start by trying some short and sweet ones, like "love," "joy" and "fun." Look at the examples, then try them for yourself in the space provided. Also, feel free to try other words, like your name, or anything else that comes to mind.

love

joy

happy

fun

you

love
joy
smile
happy

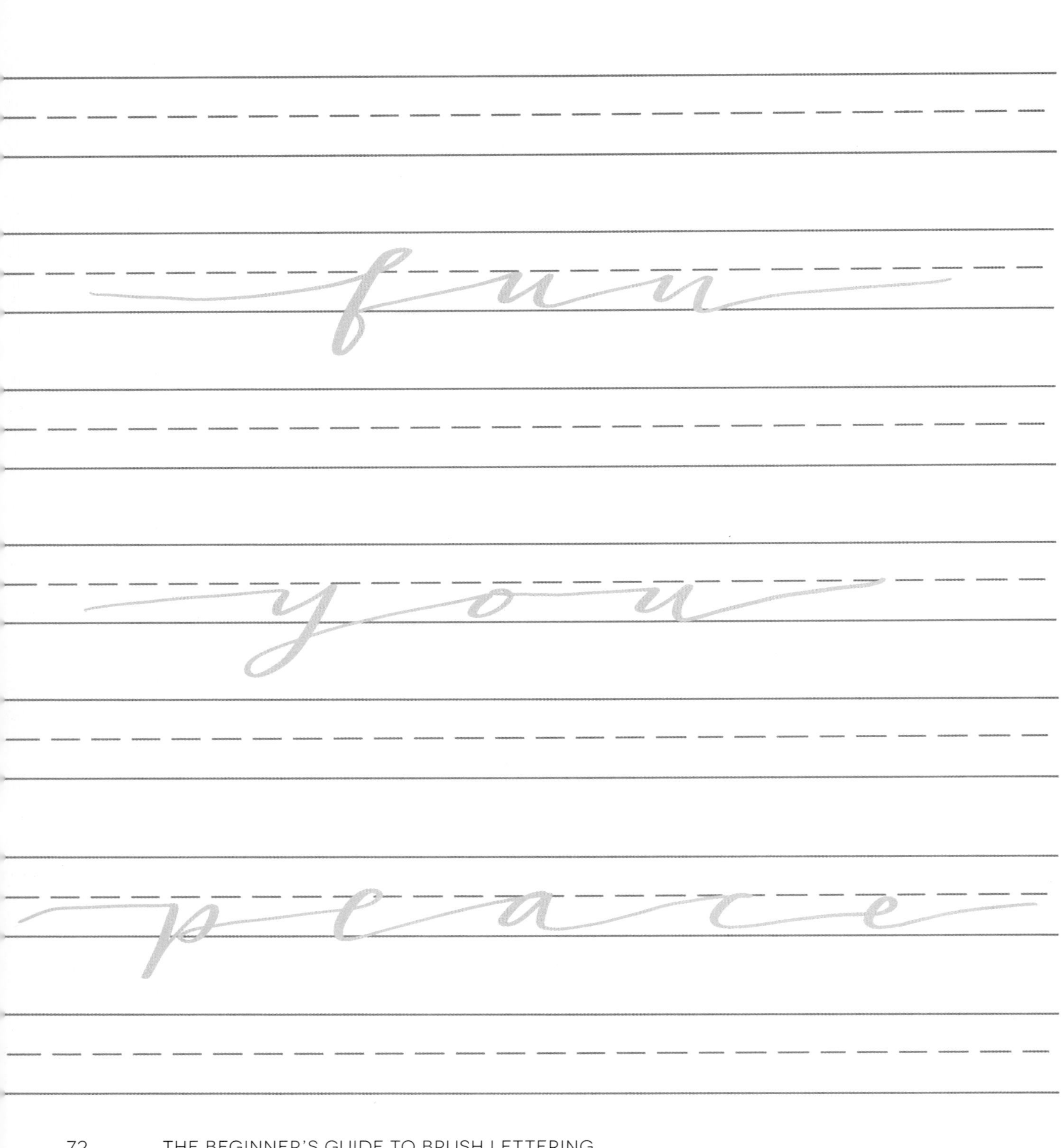
fun
you
peace

CHAPTER 7

Outlined Brush Script

Do you want your lettering to really stand out? Another fun way to take your brush script skills to the next level is by using color and adding an outline to your word after it's written. So far, we've been working exclusively with black brush pens for our practice and projects, but now we're going to use colorful brush markers to show the range of effects you can achieve with your brush lettering skills! For this lettering style, you'll need a colorful brush pen with a medium to large tip, plus a fine-tip black marker. I like to use drawing markers in the 3–5mm size range, like the Tombow MONO Drawing Pen 05. The larger the pen tip, the thicker your outline will be, so you can play around with different sizes and see what look you love most. Grab those supplies and let's get started!

First, we're going to choose a word and write it using our brush script technique (page 43). Remember to keep those downstrokes thick by applying pressure!

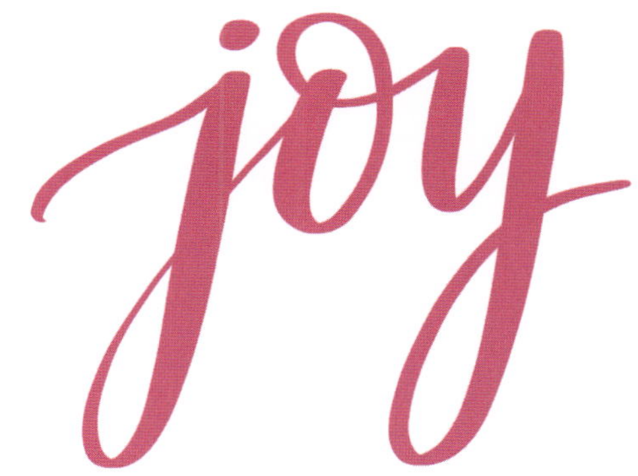

Now, we take the fine-tip marker and go back to our word, tracing all the outside edges. Don't worry if your lines aren't perfect; that's part of the beauty of handmade things.

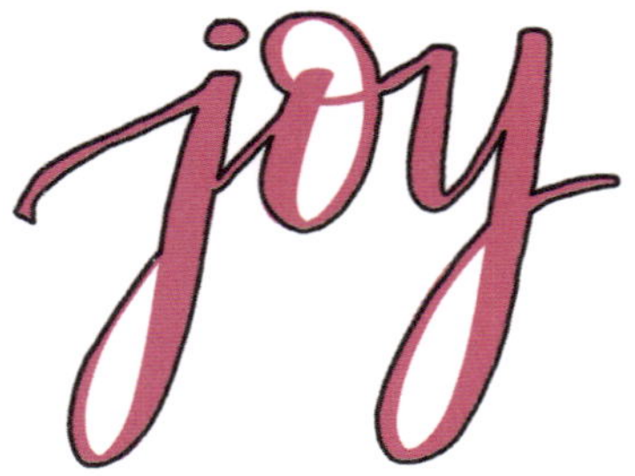

Next, go inside of any open letters and trace around the white space. This will create a complete outline of your word.

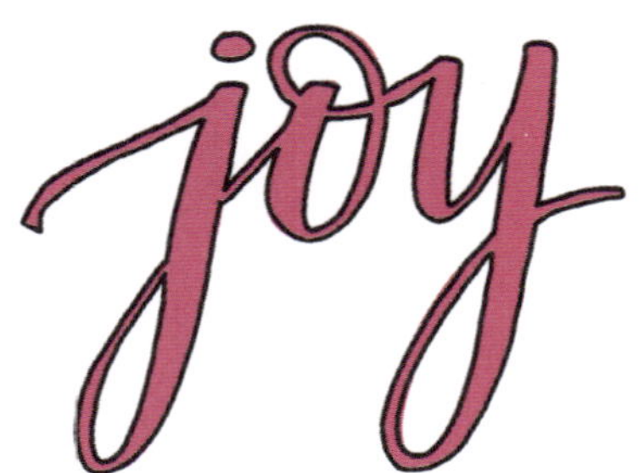

The final step is to go back and make touch-ups. Often, I'll have areas where my outline goes slightly outside the colored area, leaving a little bit of white space. To fix this, just take your colored marker and fill in any of those spaces you see.

Isn't it amazing how a little black line can make such a big difference? Another variation to try is writing in black and outlining with a colored marker. I do this far less frequently, but it definitely creates an interesting effect.

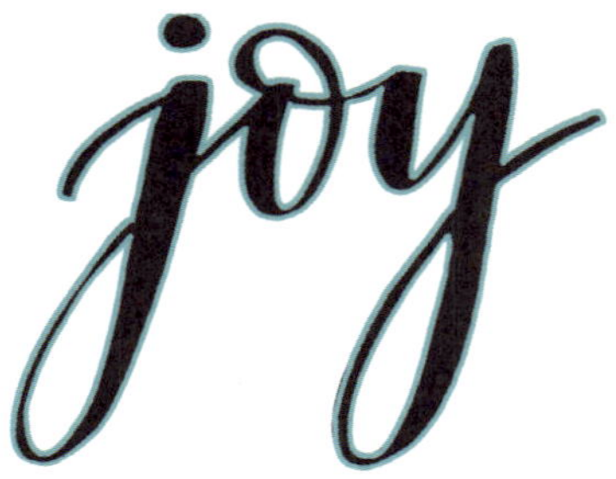

Use the space below to try this style. You can practice any words you like: Just write them with your brush pen as usual, then use the fine-tip marker to outline. This is a great way to create colorful lettering that practically pops off the page.

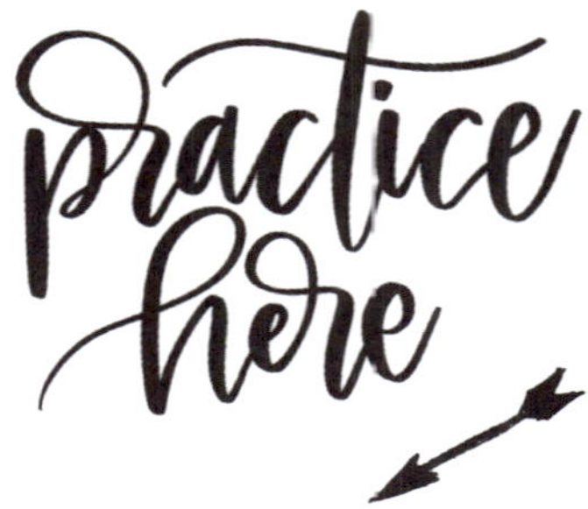

CHAPTER 8

Adding Bounce

One of my favorite things about creating is that we get to learn the rules, then break some of them on purpose because we're artists! A great example of this is taking our lettering and adding what we call "bounce." Basically, all this means is that instead of keeping our letters all neatly lined up in a row along a straight baseline, we allow them to freely move around on the page.

bounce

Some letters will be higher than others and they can even tilt in different directions. There are three main ways to achieve a "bounce" effect that's pleasing to the eye. Let's take a look at all three, then you can use one, two or all of them together in your projects as you begin to develop your own personal style.

IN-LETTER BOUNCE

Sometimes bounce can happen inside of a single letter if that letter has multiple parts; specifically, this works for "m" and "w." Instead of making the entire letter the same height, we can allow one side of the letter to drift higher than the other. In the examples below, you can see how these letters look when written normally, as well as with bounce on the left and the right sides. Not only do the different levels add visual interest, they also make these letters easier to read.

m m m

w w w

DOWNSTROKE DRIFT

When it comes to adding bounce within a word, it can be tricky figuring out which letters should be lower and which should float a little higher. The basic rule I use is that letters ending in a strong downstroke before connecting to the next letter are good spots to dip below the baseline. Some examples of letters like this are: "d," "h," "k," "l," "m," "n," "r" and "t." I let the final downstroke of these letters drift down and keep other letters higher up in the word.

practice here

TILT TECHNIQUE

In addition to letting your letters go above and below the baseline, you can also let them bounce from side to side a bit. Giving parts of a letter a gentle tilt to the left or the right can add a whimsical feel that's full of movement. Some letters lend themselves more to this than others, like letters with ascenders ("b," "d," "h," "k") and letters with multiple parts ("m" and "w").

Each of these techniques can stand alone or you can combine them for maximum bounce. There's no right or wrong amount of any of these to add to your lettered designs—it's all about your preference and how you want your project to look. We'll be attempting all three in the project section of this book to give you a feel for these different options. First, take some time to use the traceable practice pages and try out in-letter bounce, downstroke drift and tilt technique yourself. I have a feeling you're going to find bounce lettering add ctive!

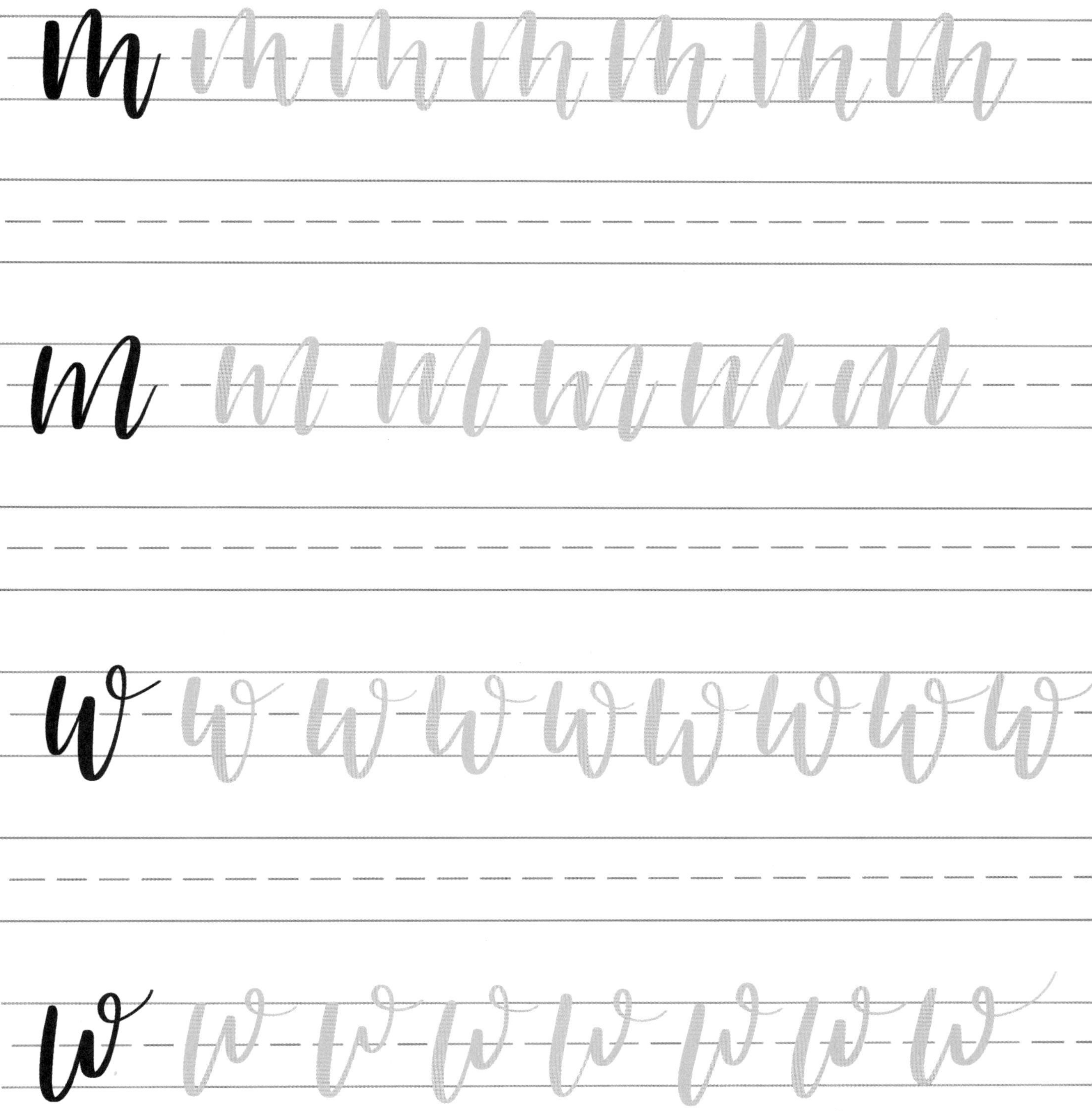

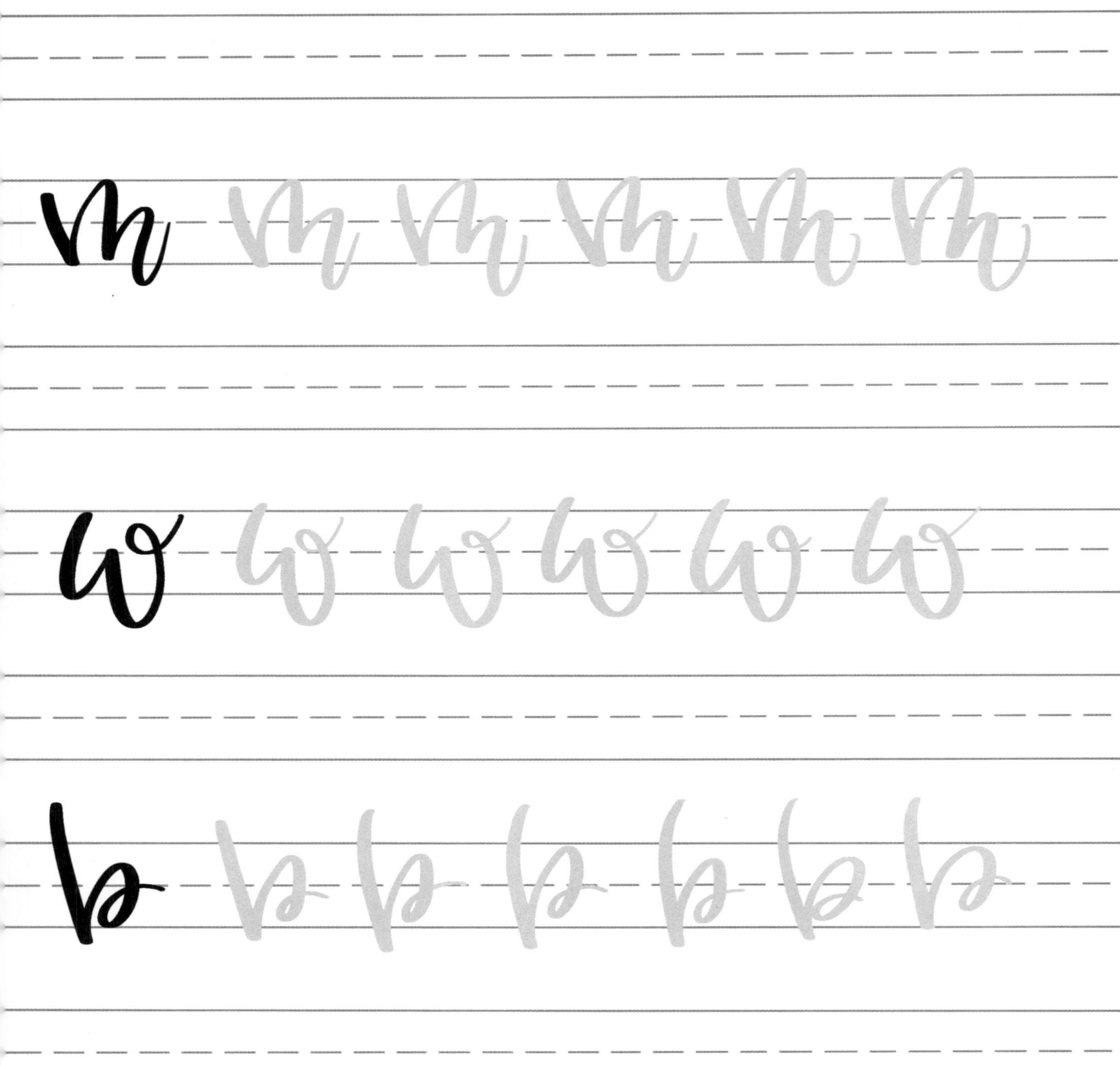

n n n n n n n n

h h h h h h h

r r r r r r r

bounce bounce

the the the

write write

letter letter

art art art

practice practice

brush pen brush

pen

Bonus Ideas

One of my favorite things about hand lettering is that there's always something new to learn. Even after you've mastered brush technique and are a pro at things like flourishes and bounce, there are other skills you can explore to take your lettering to the next level. In this book, we are focusing on brush lettering for beginners, but here are a few additional ideas you can start exploring on your own as you continue your lettering journey.

SHADOWS

Adding a drop shadow is a great way to make your lettering appear three-dimensional. To do this, I typically use a gray brush pen, like the gray Tombow Fudenosuke. I imagine a light source in the upper left corner of the page and draw gray shadows where they would naturally fall, as shown in the example below.

HIGHLIGHTS

Another technique that can enhance the appearance of your brush lettering is adding highlights. My favorite tool for this is a white gel pen (I use Uniball® Signo™). Just add a white line inside each downstroke and you'll get the effect of light shining on your letters and causing parts of them to glow.

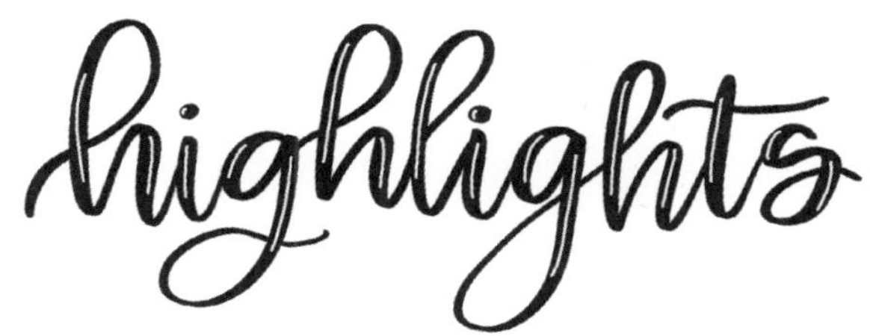

DOTS

Using dots is a great way to add some texture to your lettering. In the example below, I've used white dots (once again, a gel pen is a great choice) in the bottom section of each downstroke. This adds visual interest and an interesting effect. If your letters are written in a different color, you can use any color dots you like. You can also choose to fill the entire downstroke rather than just a portion of it. Try a few variations and see what you like best.

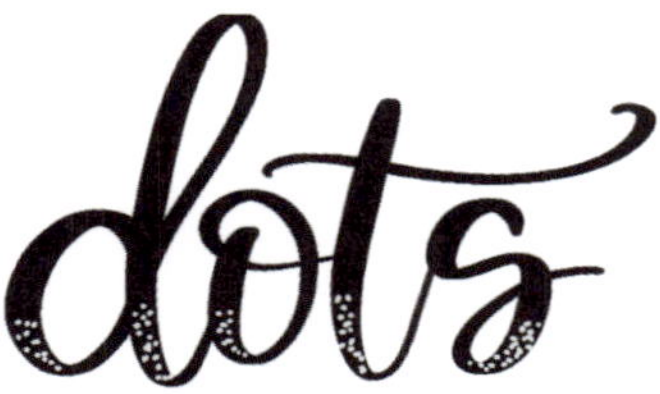

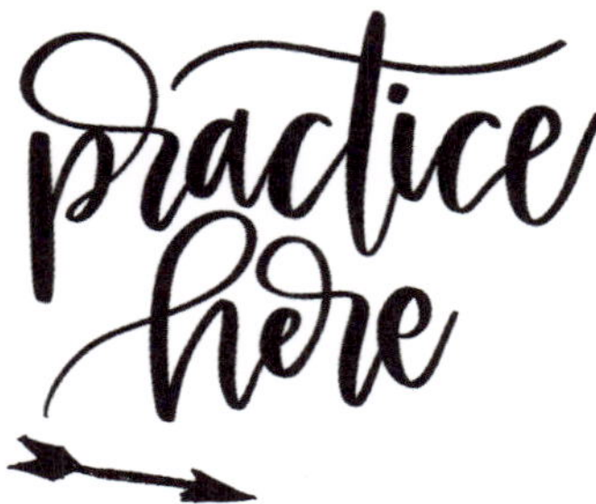

BLENDING

If you're using colored markers for your brush lettering, blending two or more shades together can really make your words pop. I like to write an entire word in one color first, then go back and retrace over just the bottom half using a darker pen. This creates a fun ombré effect and also gives your letters some dimension.

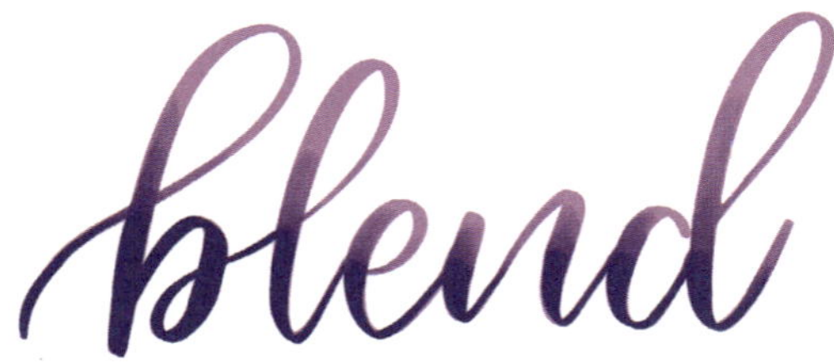

These are just a few of the many ways you can experiment with brush lettering. I haven't included any of them in the projects we will be completing because I wanted to keep those somewhat simple, but feel free to add them into the designs yourself if you choose!

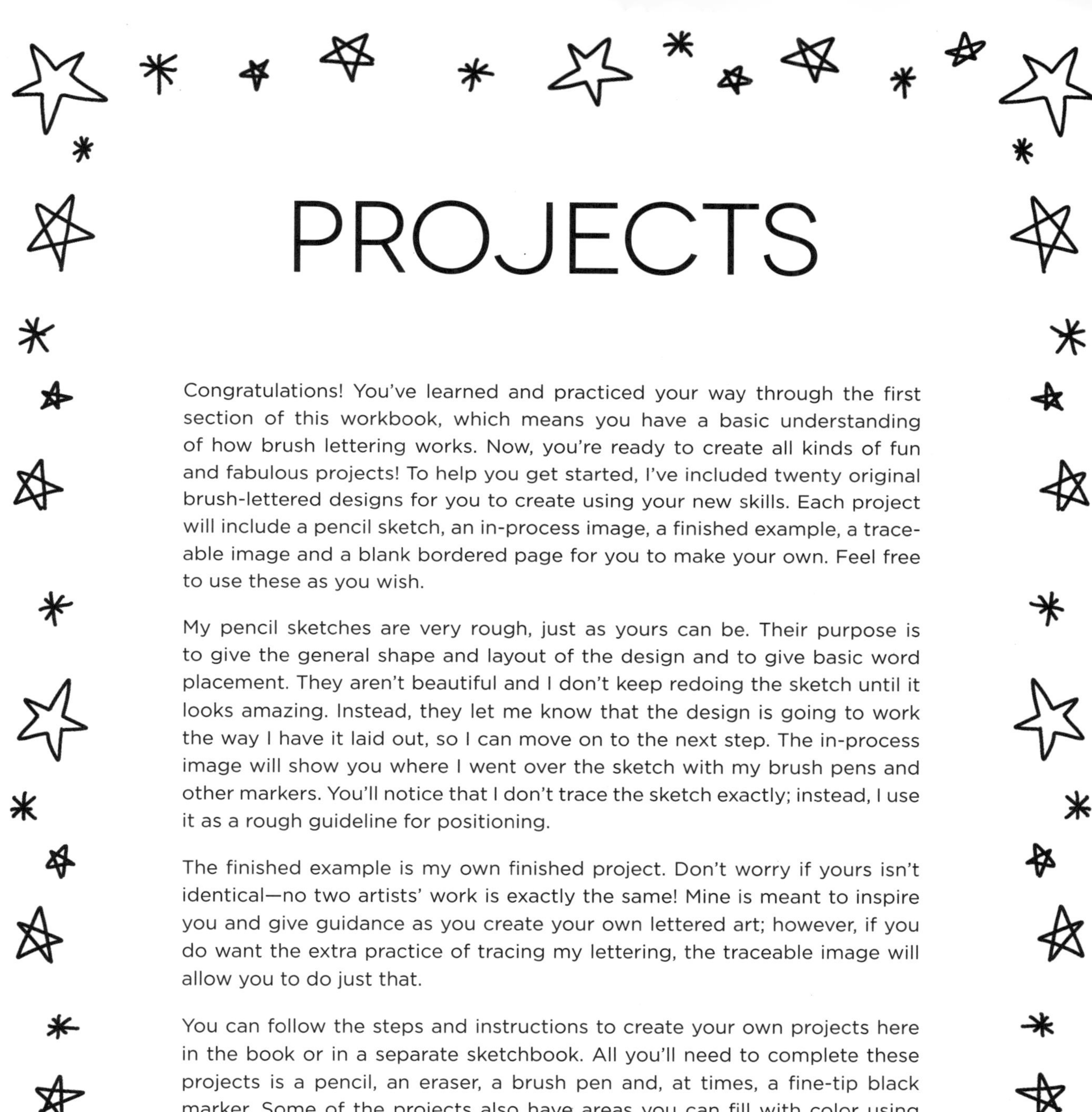

PROJECTS

Congratulations! You've learned and practiced your way through the first section of this workbook, which means you have a basic understanding of how brush lettering works. Now, you're ready to create all kinds of fun and fabulous projects! To help you get started, I've included twenty original brush-lettered designs for you to create using your new skills. Each project will include a pencil sketch, an in-process image, a finished example, a traceable image and a blank bordered page for you to make your own. Feel free to use these as you wish.

My pencil sketches are very rough, just as yours can be. Their purpose is to give the general shape and layout of the design and to give basic word placement. They aren't beautiful and I don't keep redoing the sketch until it looks amazing. Instead, they let me know that the design is going to work the way I have it laid out, so I can move on to the next step. The in-process image will show you where I went over the sketch with my brush pens and other markers. You'll notice that I don't trace the sketch exactly; instead, I use it as a rough guideline for positioning.

The finished example is my own finished project. Don't worry if yours isn't identical—no two artists' work is exactly the same! Mine is meant to inspire you and give guidance as you create your own lettered art; however, if you do want the extra practice of tracing my lettering, the traceable image will allow you to do just that.

You can follow the steps and instructions to create your own projects here in the book or in a separate sketchbook. All you'll need to complete these projects is a pencil, an eraser, a brush pen and, at times, a fine-tip black marker. Some of the projects also have areas you can fill with color using your favorite markers, colored pencils or watercolors for a finishing touch. Ready? Let's start creating!

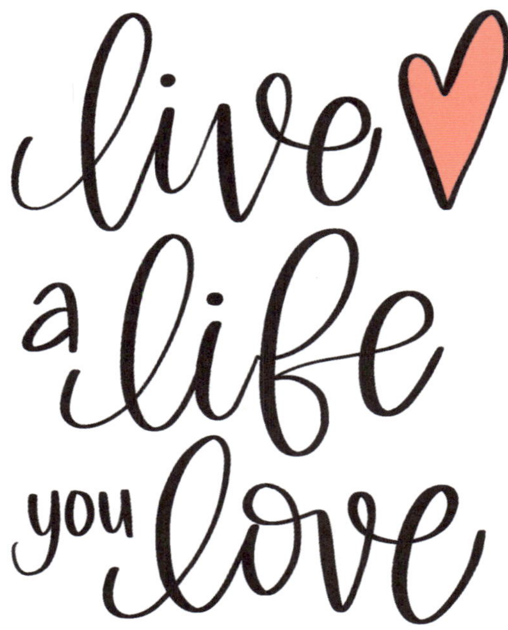

For our first project, we're going to start nice and simple with the quote "live a life you love." After all, we only get one life, so we might as well enjoy it, right? Pursue those passions, do what you love and spend time with the people who mean the most to you. We can't control everything, but when we do have decisions to make, building a life we actually enjoy is a great direction to take. As we go further in our workbook, we'll be working with shaped images, embellishments and other more advanced skills, but, for now, let's focus on just the lettering itself and making it look great! Let's get started.

The first step in lettering our project is that we're going to split this phrase into three straight lines of text. Our finished image will be a rectangular shape, so this is perfect for creating on a canvas or on a piece of Bristol board for framing. First, you'll want to use a pencil to sketch the positions of the three main words: "live," "life" and "love." Start with "live" slightly to the left of the rectangle, then let each of the other words drift slightly to the right. Then, print the other words in pencil. I made these smaller than the words I wanted to emphasize. Combining brush script with a simple print adds visual interest. It also gives the artist a way to make the most important words (the ones in script) stand out, while the others fade into the background a bit. Finally, sketch a heart in the top right corner of the design.

Now, it's time to bring out the brush pen. If you're working on canvas, I recommend something permanent like the Tombow ABT PRO Alcohol-Based Markers. If you're using paper or Bristol board, any brush marker will do. Trace over your penciled letters, remembering to apply pressure to every downstroke in the script words.

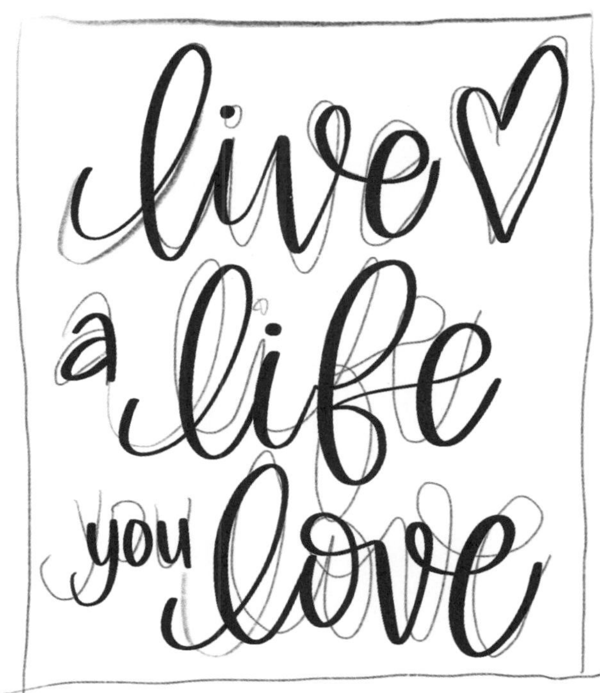

When you're finished, allow the ink to dry completely, then erase any pencil marks you can still see. Fill in your heart with color and your design will be complete!

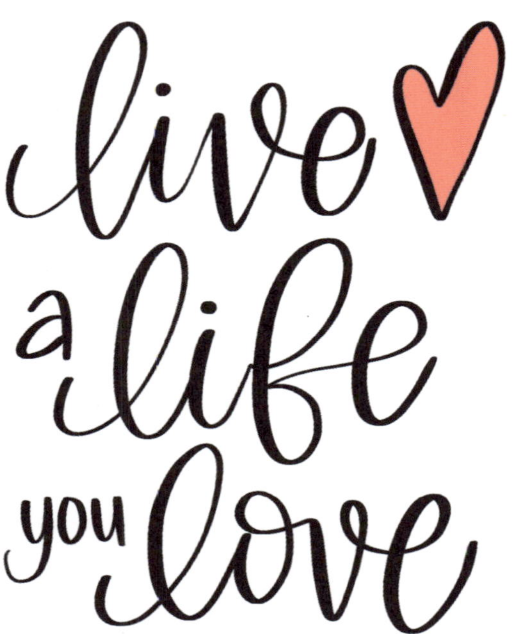

Here's a traceable version you can use to practice; then it's your turn to create your own.

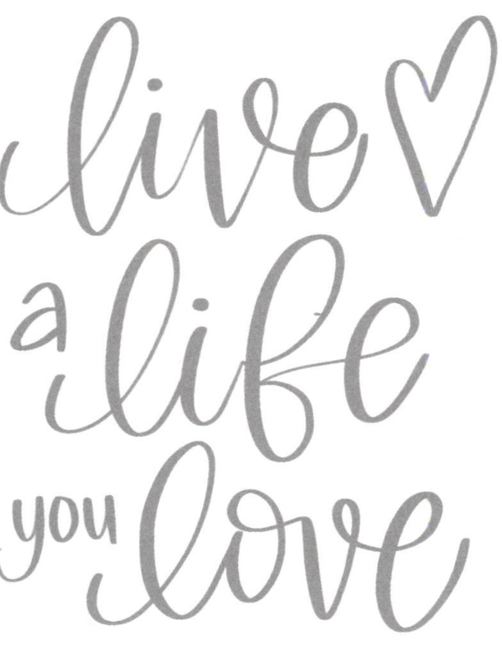

PROJECT 2

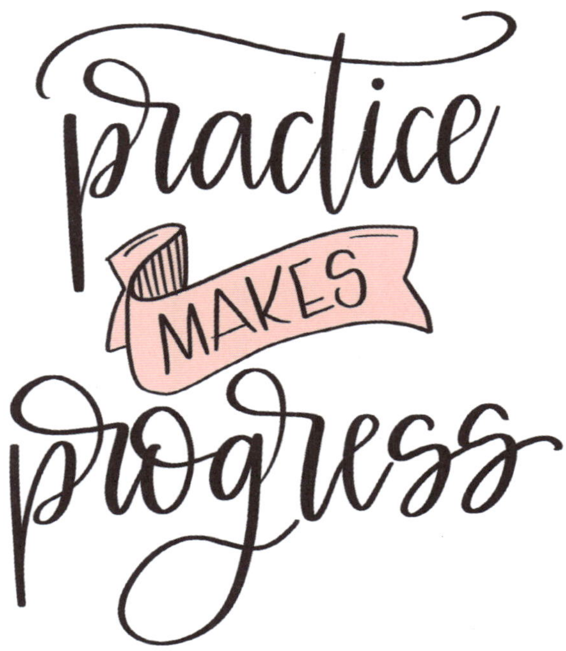

Here's another beginner-level project that uses three lines of text, but this time we're incorporating a fun decorative element: the banner! The quote we're lettering, "practice makes progress," is a personal favorite of mine; in fact, if you've ever met me in person, taken one of my online classes or read another of my books, you know that it's my main motto. In lettering (and in life), we are never going to be perfect, so, when that's our expectation, we're setting ourselves up for frustration and disappointment. But, the great reality is that the more we practice something, the better we'll become. If we put in time and effort, we'll always see progress—and that's something to celebrate!

To letter this quote, we're going to use our brush script to emphasize the words "practice" and "progress," then join them together with the printed word "MAKES" inside our doodle. The first step is to use a pencil to sketch three horizontal lines. Then, sketch the positions of the first and last words. In the center, you'll draw a banner. To do this, draw a rounded "z" shape, then use the example below (and in the traceable design) to help you create the rest of the shape. Print the word "MAKES" inside the banner.

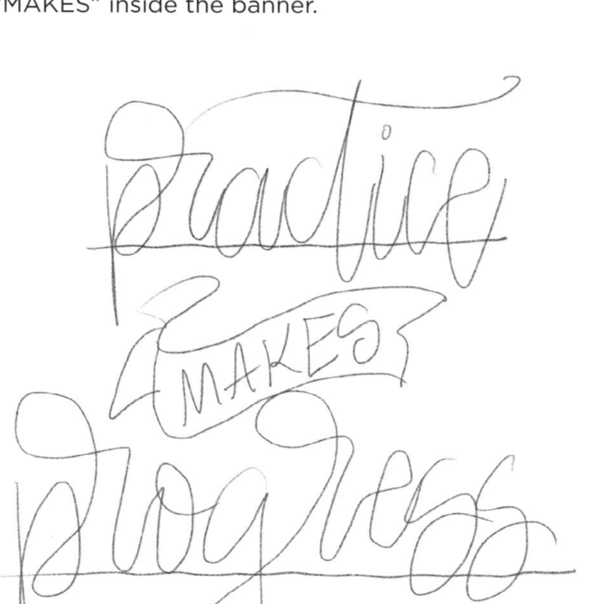

Now, use your brush pen to letter the words "practice" and "progress" over the top of your sketches. Remember to apply pressure anytime your pen is moving down on the page. Trace over the banner and the final word using a pigment-based brush pen or a fine-line drawing pen. If you use a water-based marker for this last step, it will bleed if you try to color the banner later.

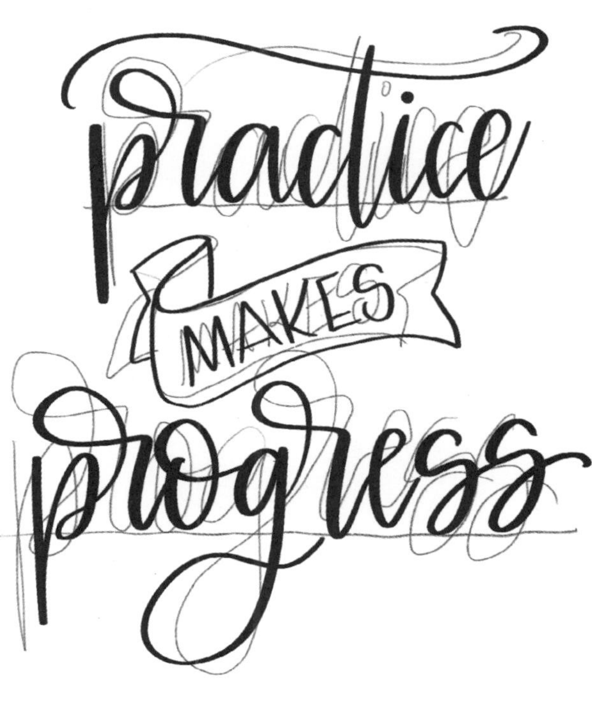

Once the ink is dry, it's time to erase the pencil lines. This is a great time to add embellishments like detail lines on the banner and in the fold.

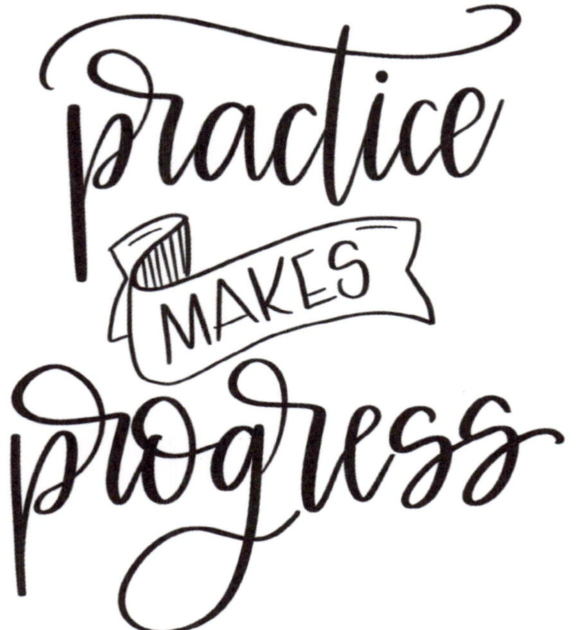

To take your project to the next level, now you can color in the banner. I recommend using a light color so that your lettering is still easy to read.

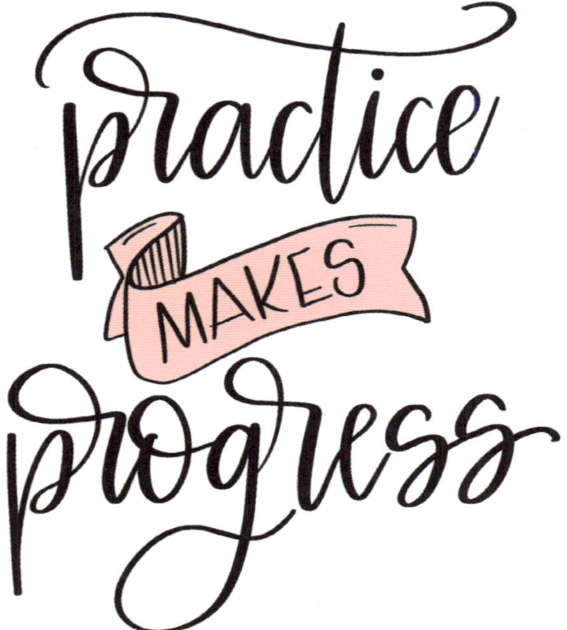

Ready to try it? Here's a traceable image to help you master the banner (and the lettering). Then, it's your turn to create your own version of this design on the provided bordered page.

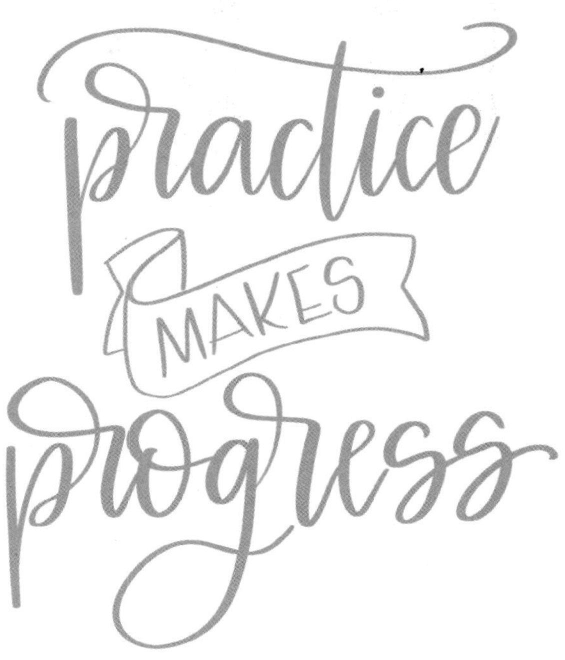

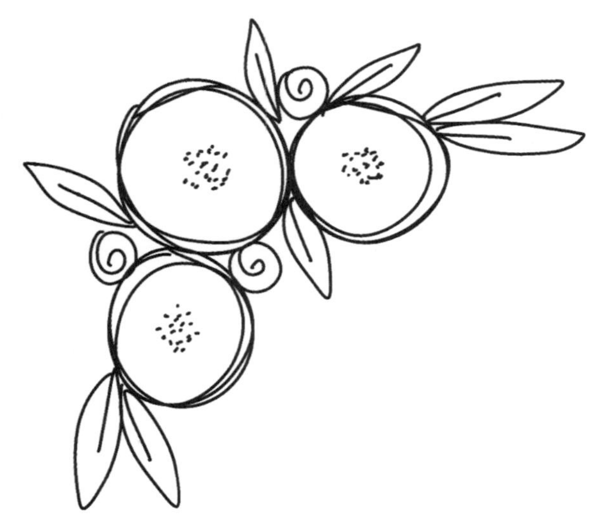

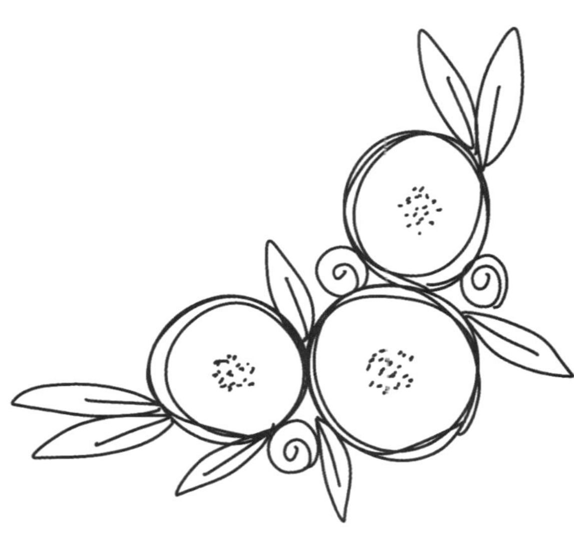

PROJECT 3

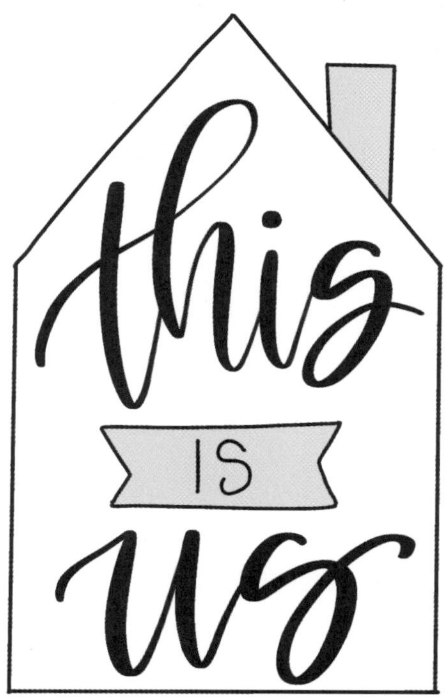

One of the most challenging things about creating a lettered project is figuring out how you want to lay out the design. The easiest method is splitting the text into several straight lines, as we did in our first two projects together. For the quote "this is us," we're going to do that again, but instead of stopping there, we'll take this design up a notch by placing it inside a larger shape: a house! It's the perfect choice for a shape because the phrase is so often used in home décor. It's a sweet sentiment to hang on the wall, which you can easily do if you frame your completed project. You can also practice the design, then re-create it with fabric markers on a pillow or paint pens on a wooden sign.

The first step is to sketch the word placement in pencil. The words "this" and "us" will be in brush script, with the printed word "IS" in between. We're going to use a different style of banner around the center word: a simple rectangle with a sideways "v" on each side. Once we have the word placement, it's time to sketch a simple house shape around the phrase. I added a little chimney on the top right just for fun.

The next step in our project is to use a brush pen to letter the script words. You'll notice that in my example, I let the "t" drift a little lower and the "h" sits a little higher for just a bit of bounce (see page 75 for details on bounce technique). I also used the crossbar of the "t" to go right into the loop of the "h," creating a fun little flourish. Next, use a fine-tip marker (I use a Tombow MONO Drawing Pen) to trace the banner and the third word.

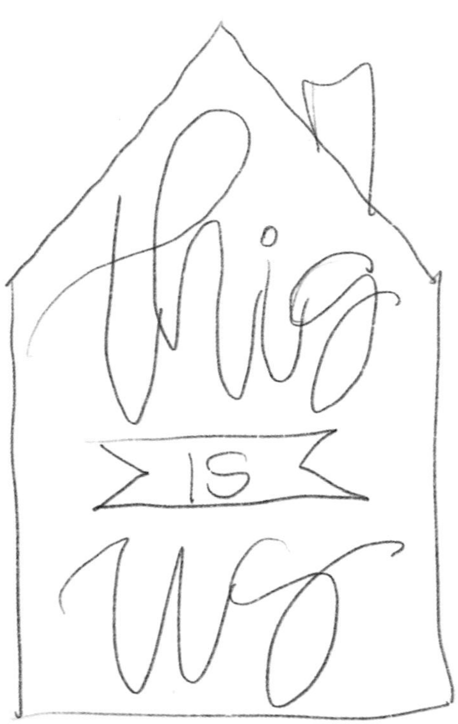

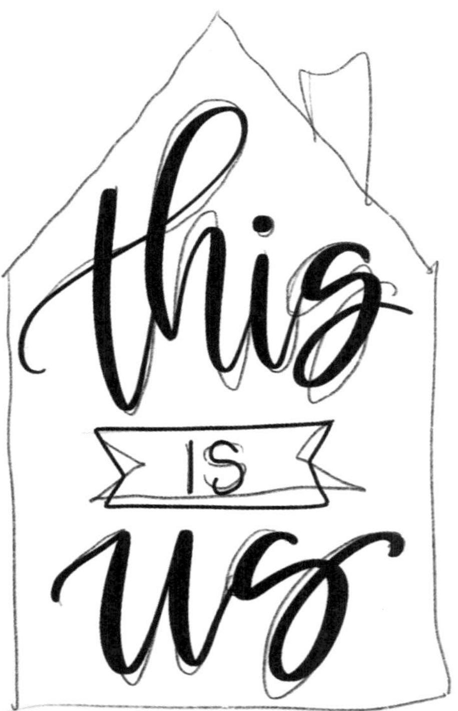

With the same fine-tip marker, use a ruler or straight-edge tool to trace the outline of the house and the chimney.

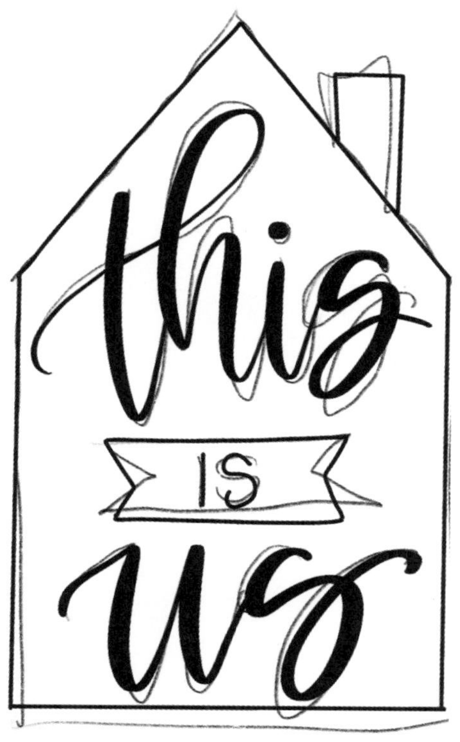

Now, it's time to erase any remaining pencil marks to reveal our beautiful design! Make sure you allow the ink enough time to dry so that there are no smudges to mar your work.

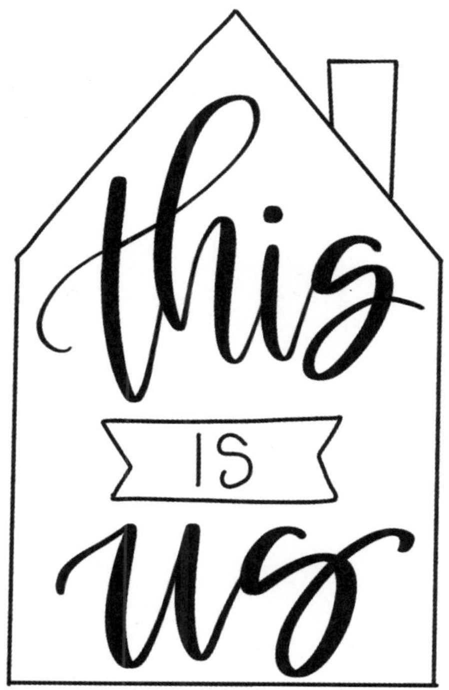

The final step for this project is to add a bit of color. I colored in my banner and the chimney just to make the design pop. You can also color in the entire house shape if you like.

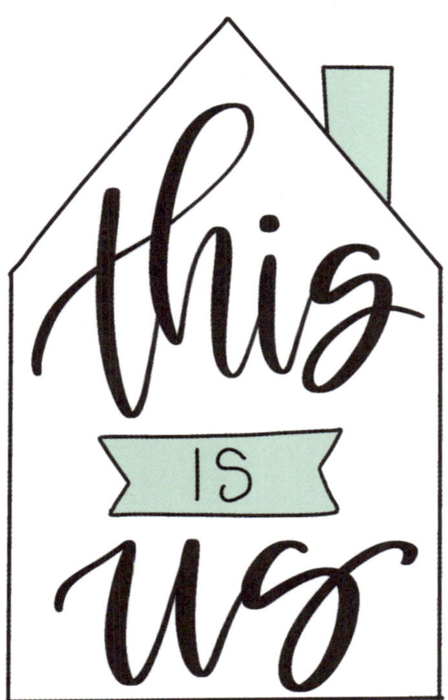

This is a simple way to dive into the world of shaped designs, which we'll be exploring in more of our coming projects. But first, here's a traceable image to get you ready to try this one on your own. Once you're feeling confident, go ahead and create your own project on any surface you like! Remember, if you're lettering on a non-paper surface, you'll want to use alcohol-based markers so your work is permanent.

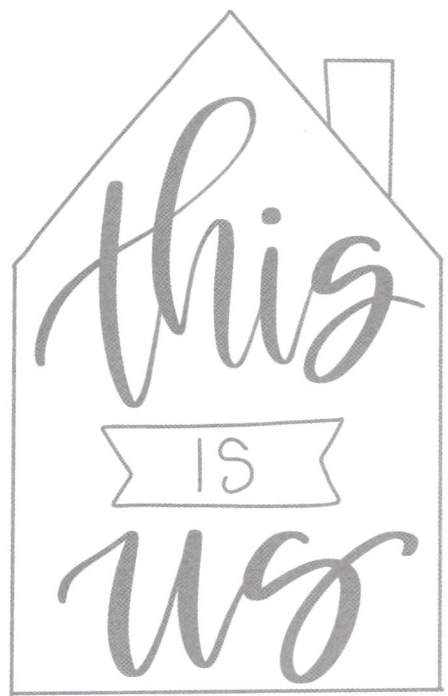

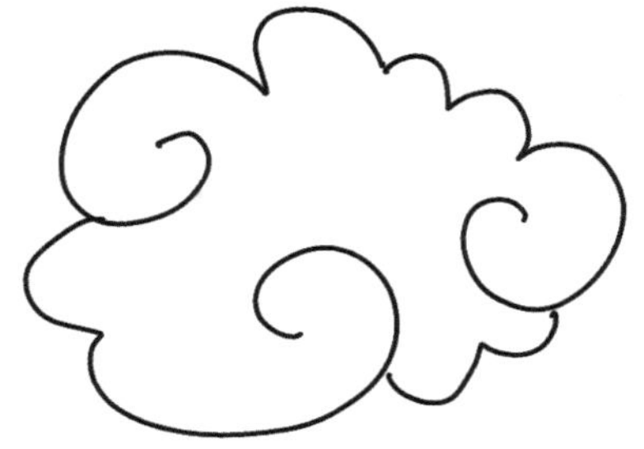

PROJECT 4

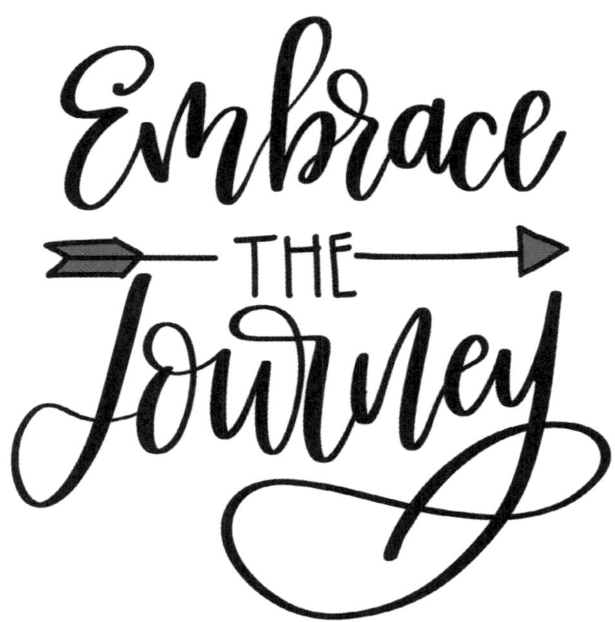

This next project gives us a chance to experiment with using all three types of bounce (page 75), as well as a fun flourish—an arrow. We'll be lettering "Embrace THE Journey" using a simple layout with one word per line. Although the quote is simple, it's a great reminder that even when we're not quite where we want to be, it's important to be present right where we are. Whether it's in work, in a relationship or in some other aspect of life, we learn far more along the journey than we would if we just ended up at our desired destination right away! This quote can be an encouragement for anyone and would be a great addition to an office or a kids' room.

First, use a pencil to sketch the positions of the words, writing "Embrace" and "Journey" in script for the top and bottom lines. In between, print "THE" and draw half an arrow on either side.

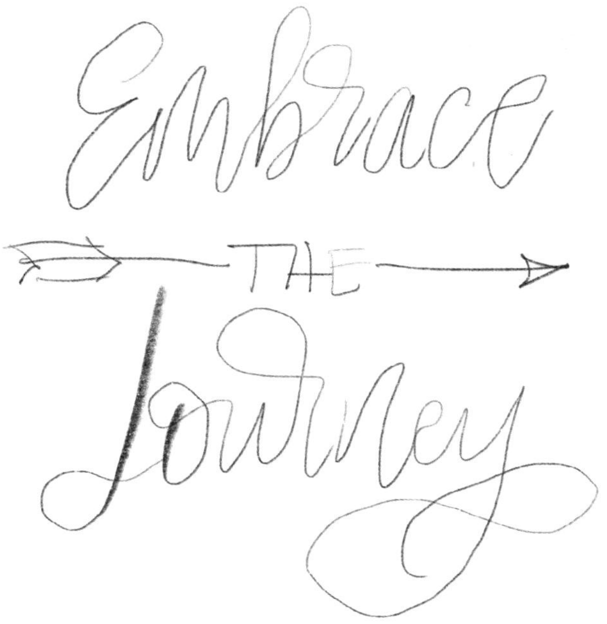

Once you have a sketch, it's time to trace over your words. Use a brush pen to letter "Embrace" and "Journey," making sure to apply pressure to the downstrokes. I used some in-letter bounce, as well as a bit of tilt, to make the words feel whimsical. Then, trace "THE" along with the arrow using a fine-tip black marker. You may want to use a straight edge to help you keep the lines of the arrow straight.

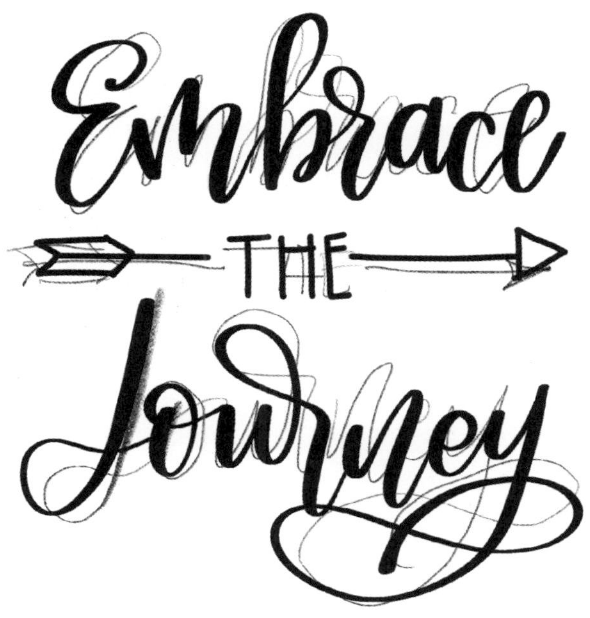

To make your design pop, you can color the arrow with any marker you like. I chose purple, but you can personalize yours with your own favorite color. Erase any remaining pencil lines that are visible and your project will be complete.

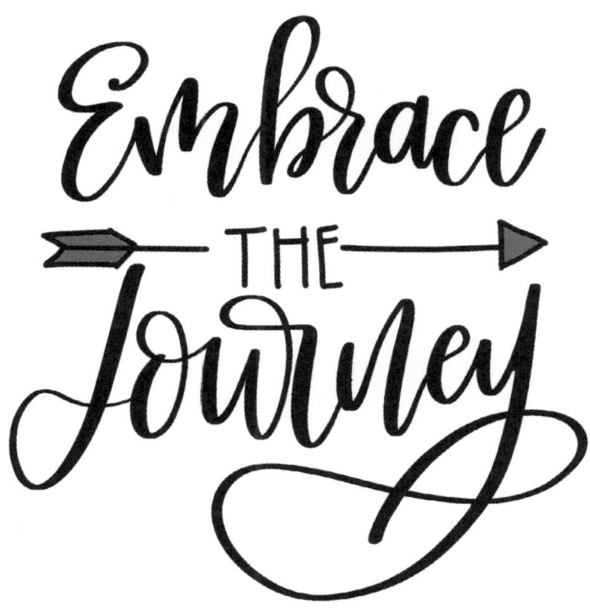

If you'd like to practice by tracing my sample design, you can do so using the image below. Then, turn to the page bordered with arrows and give it a try on your own!

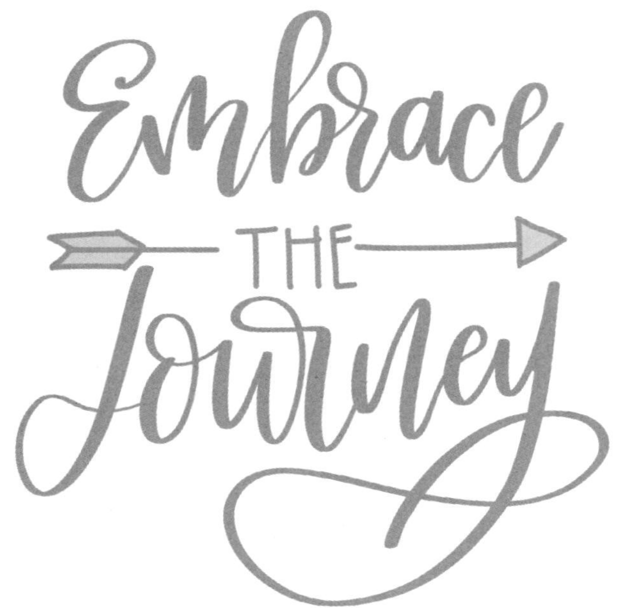

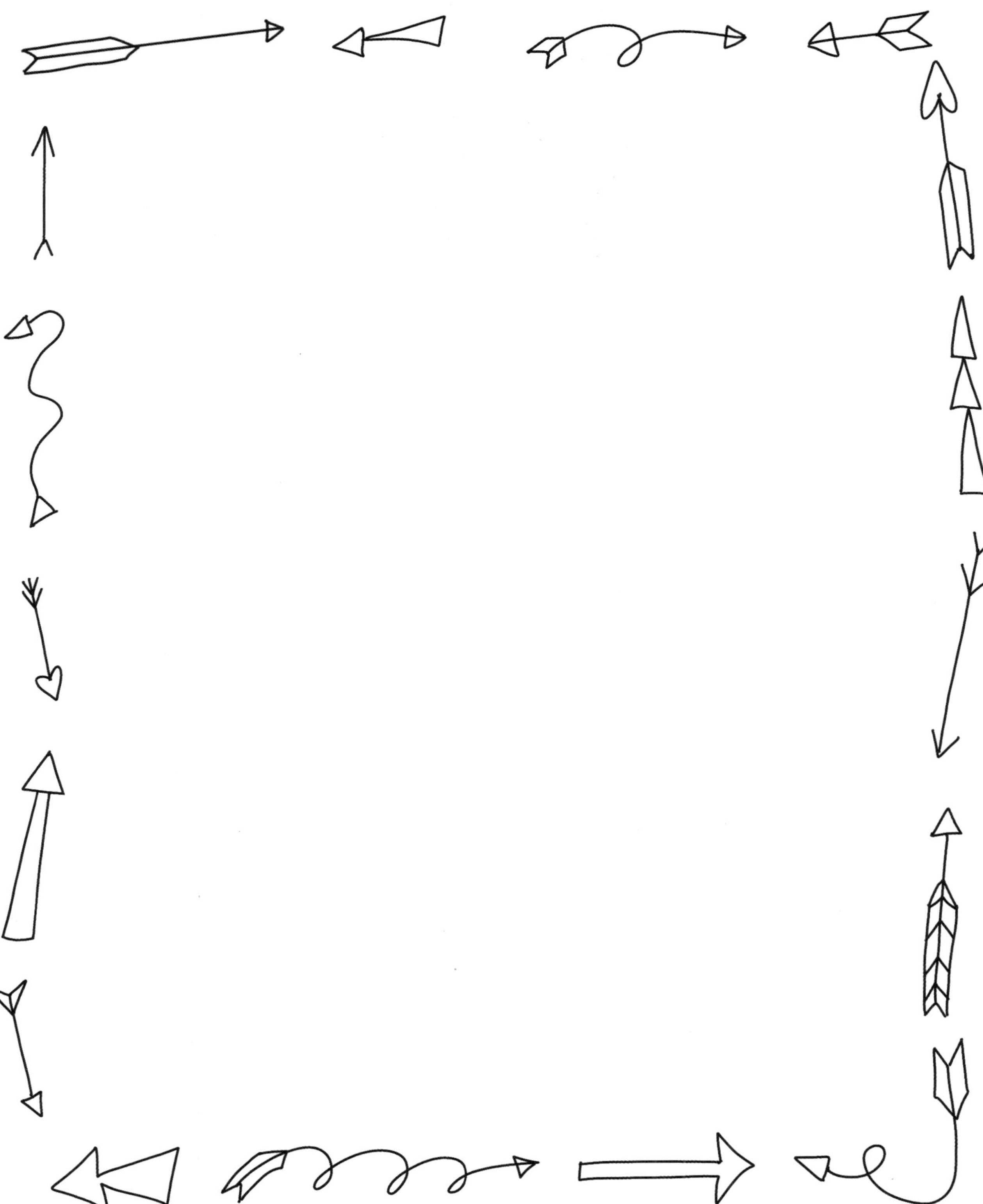

PROJECT 5

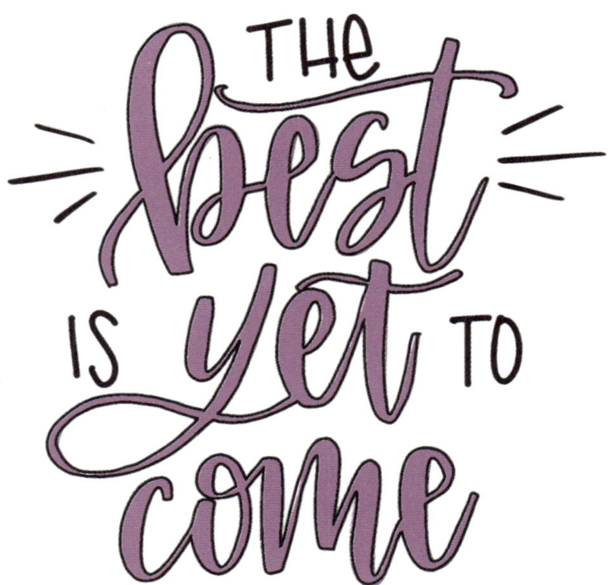

Now that you've got a few projects under your belt, it's time to try lettering a slightly longer phrase. We're also going to incorporate the outlining technique we learned in Chapter 7 (page 73). Ready? Grab your pencil and let's get started. First, sketch the position of your words. I stacked mine in four lines. I printed the small connecting words—"THE," "IS" and "TO"—while the rest are written in brush script.

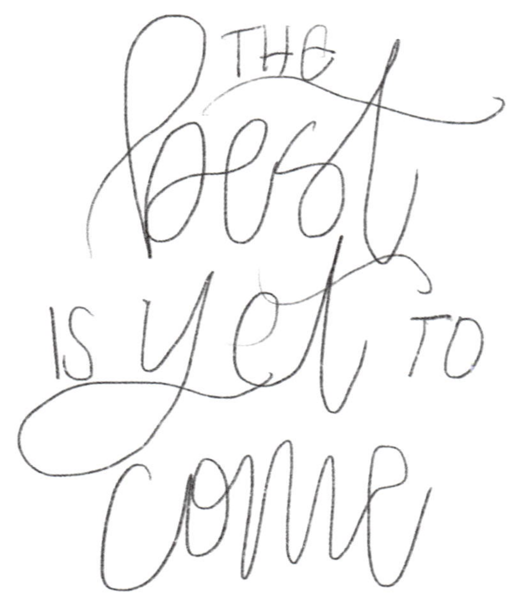

Next, it's time to do our lettering using a colorful marker. Choose any color brush pen you like and use the brush technique to write the words "best," "yet" and "come," making sure to apply pressure on every downstroke. Remember, you want to use a pen with a medium or large tip so you have plenty of colored area to outline later. Then, use a fine-tip black marker to write the rest of the words.

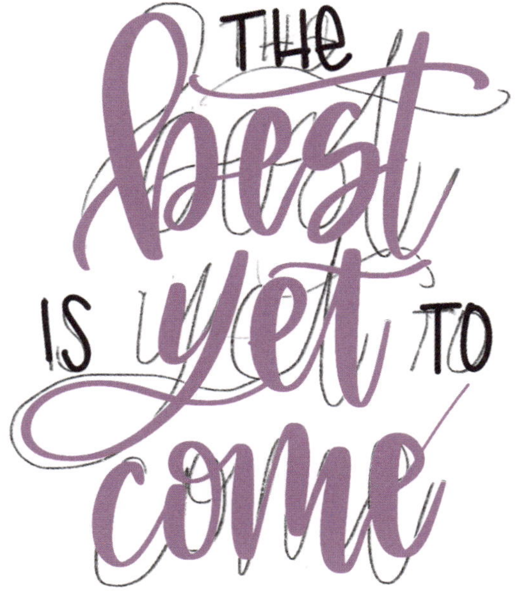

Using the same fine-tip black marker, carefully trace the outer edges of the brush-lettered words, as well as any open spaces on the insides of letters like "b" and "e." Add a few accent lines on either side of "best" to draw the viewer's eye, then erase any pencil marks to finish your project.

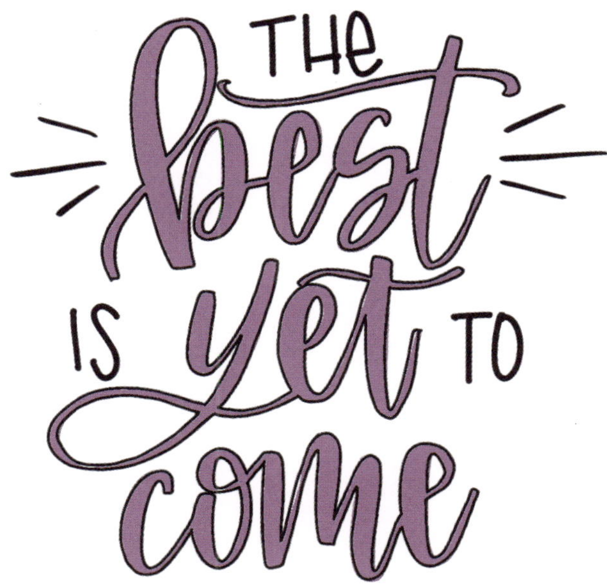

Feel free to trace the design below to get yourself warmed up, then try lettering it on your own! The page with daisies on the sides is a perfect spot to create your finished project.

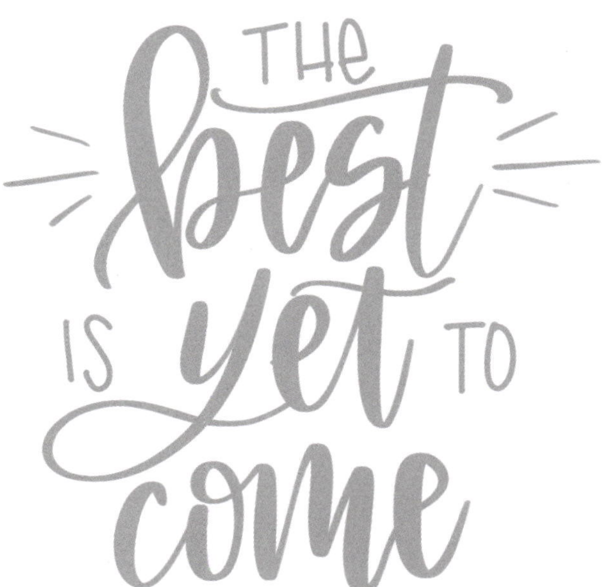

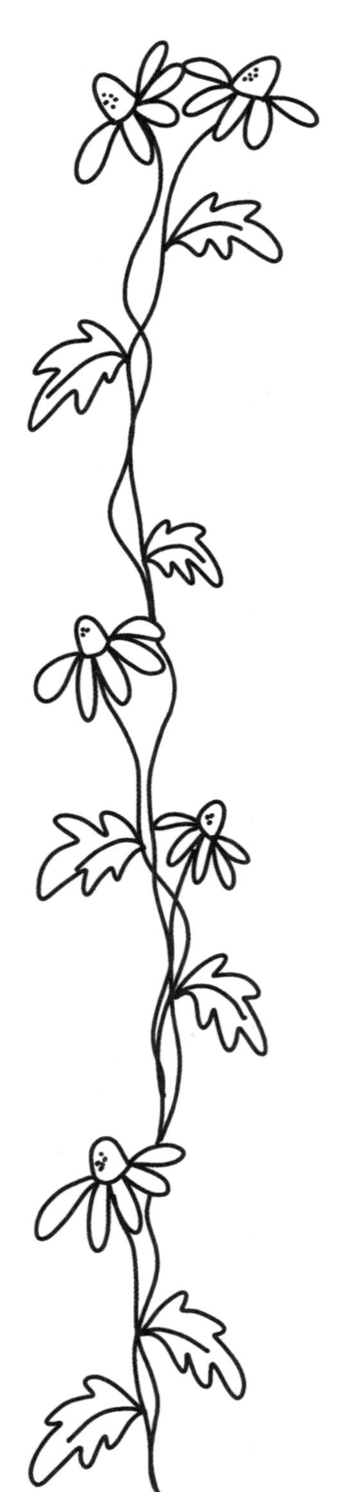

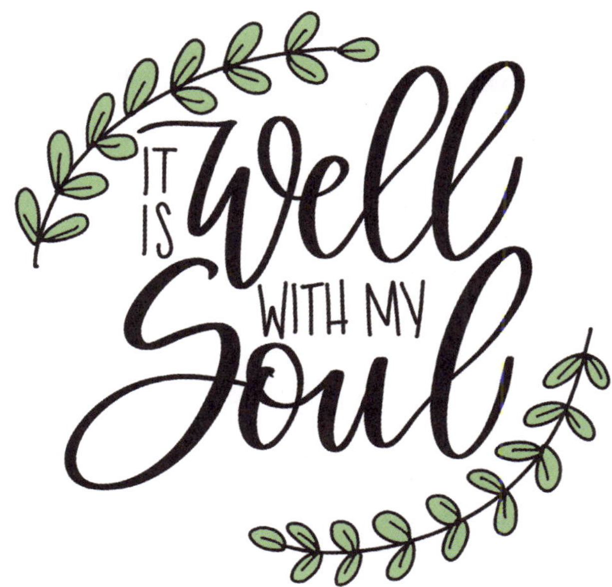

This next project gives us a chance to bring in some botanicals and nature elements, by framing our phrase with some leafy vines. Flowers and leaves are great embellishments to learn because they're appropriate to use with just about any phrase you might want to letter. Natural elements bring color and life to a design, as well as beauty. For our project, I chose the quote "IT IS Well WITH MY Soul," which reminds us that even in circumstances that are less than ideal, we can still find peace and joy.

First, sketch your word placement in pencil. I started with the word “Well” in large script, then wrote “Soul” below it, making sure there was a little bit of space in between the two words. Then, I filled in the remaining words with smaller printed letters. Once the phrase is sketched, draw two arching lines around it: one around the top left portion and one around the bottom right area.

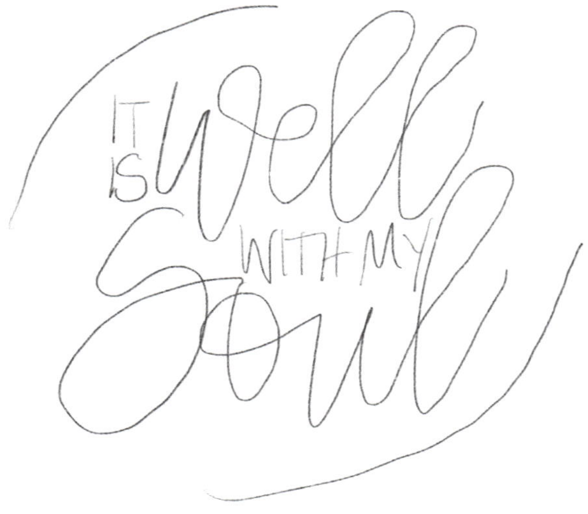

Use your brush pen to letter the script words, making sure to apply pressure to thicken the downstrokes in each letter. Then, use a fine-tip black marker to trace the printed words and the arches. The arches will be the stems of your leafy vines. Now, draw small teardrop-shaped leaves along the stems, adding a small vein inside each leaf.

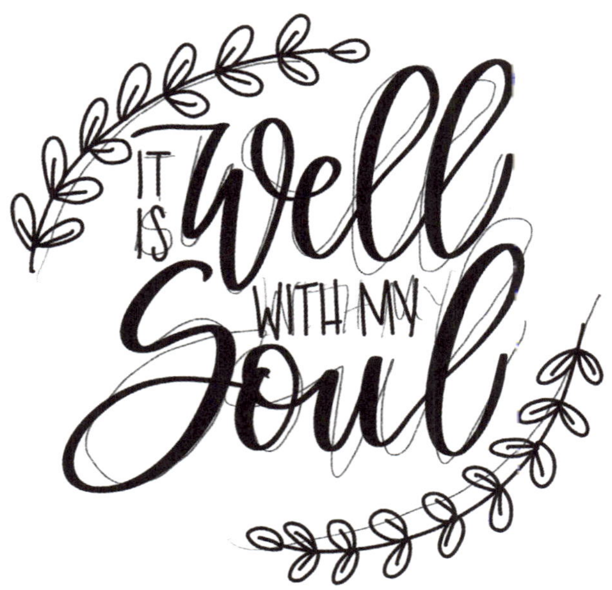

Erase any pencil lines you can still see, then color your leaves to complete the project. I chose to make mine green, but you can also use fall leaf colors, too, like red, orange and yellow.

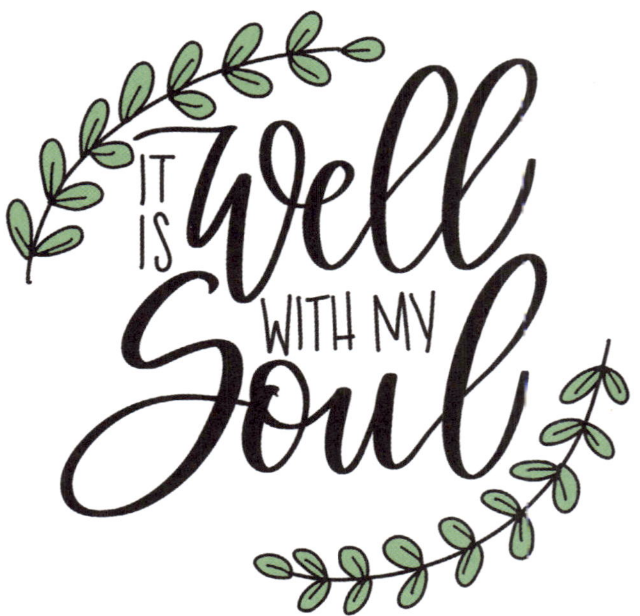

Use the image below to trace the design if you like, then it's time to create your own version on the page bordered with more leafy vines. As always, feel free to change anything about the project to put an original spin on it.

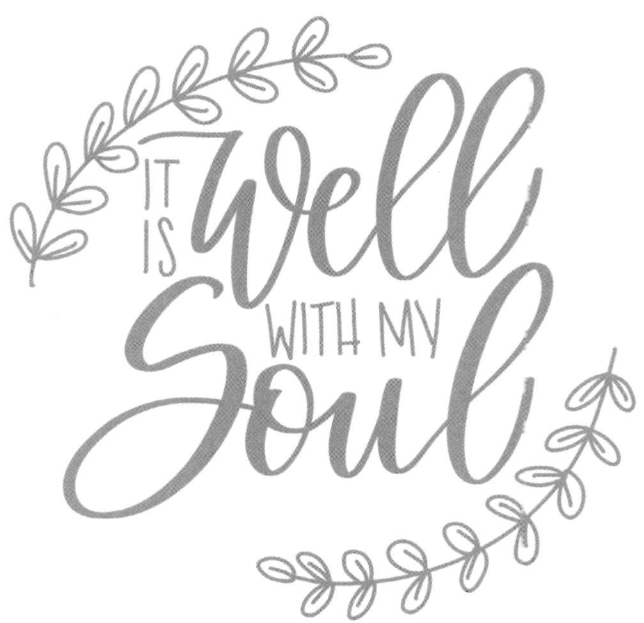

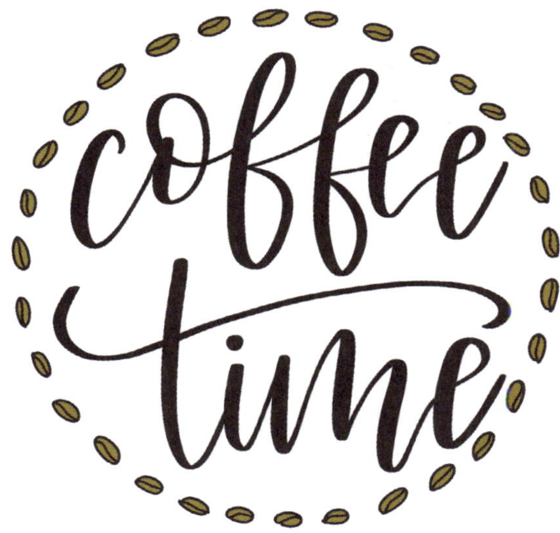

It's time to try a new kind of shaped design! We're going to put our words inside a circle for this coffee-themed project. I'm personally a huge fan of all kinds of coffee, particularly when it's iced and flavored with mocha or caramel. So, I enjoy lettering lots of coffee phrases, many of which are on the walls of my kitchen and dining room; however, if you're not a big coffee drinker, feel free to substitute tea or your own beverage of choice into the design. This project looks adorable framed and displayed on a kitchen shelf, or you can even use a paint marker to letter on tile coasters.

The first step is to sketch or trace a circle in pencil. I like to use the lid of a jar or a small bowl for tracing mine. Then, sketch the words "coffee time" inside. Try to let the letters bounce in a way that fills up the space (see page 75 for details on bounce technique).

Next, use your brush pen to do the lettering, pressing on the downstrokes and releasing pressure everywhere else.

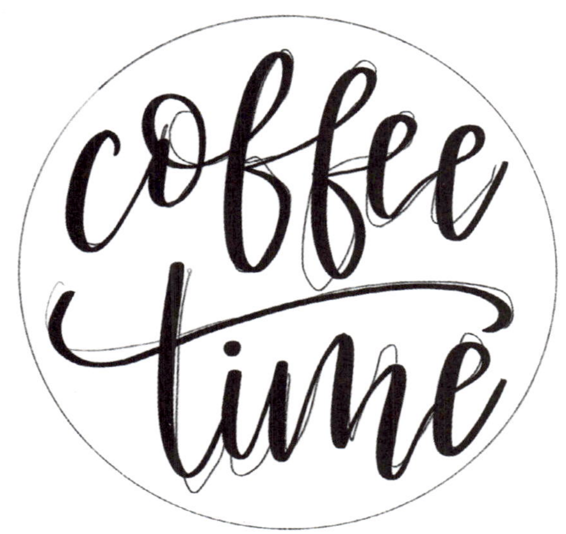

To border your words, draw a series of small coffee beans (ovals with a line through the center) all around the original circle. You can use your brush pen or a small drawing marker for this step. If you've substituted another beverage for coffee, you can swap out the beans for round polka dots or even the leafy vines from the previous project.

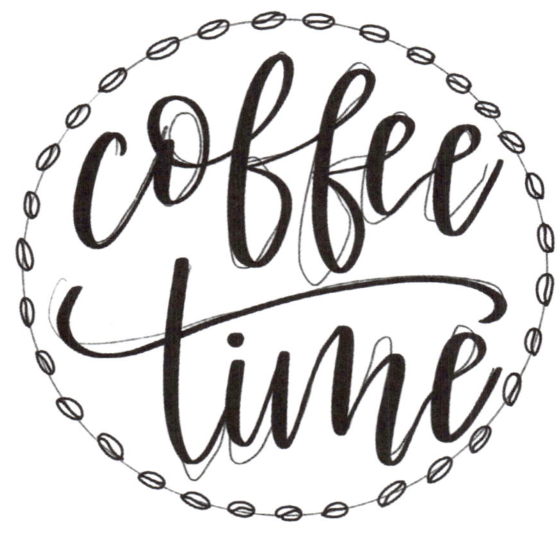

Erase any visible pencil lines, then color your coffee beans brown to complete the project.

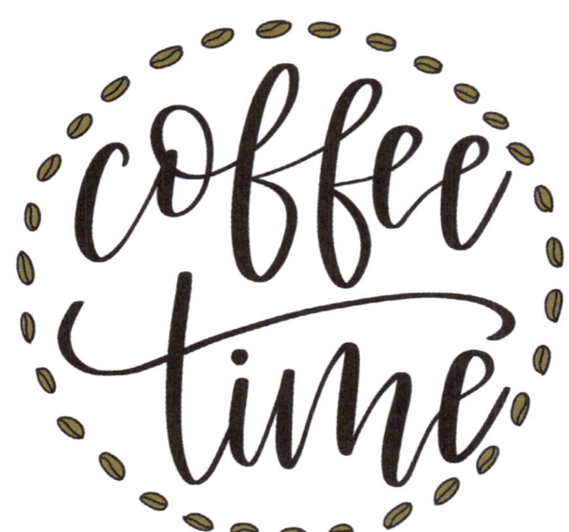

Feel free to trace the design below for extra practice before trying it on your own. The page bordered with coffee cups is ready to be colored and filled in with your unique project.

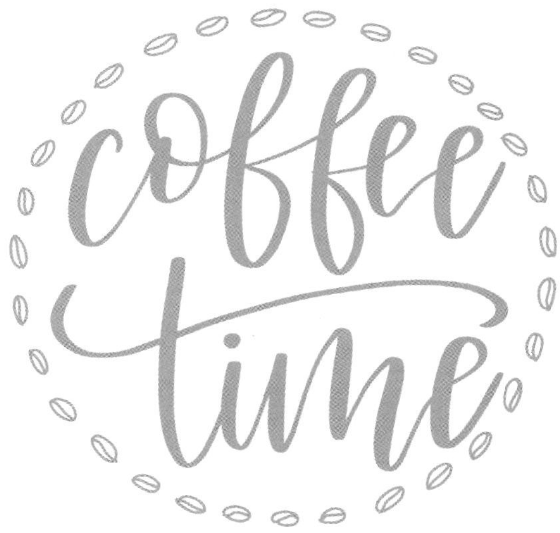

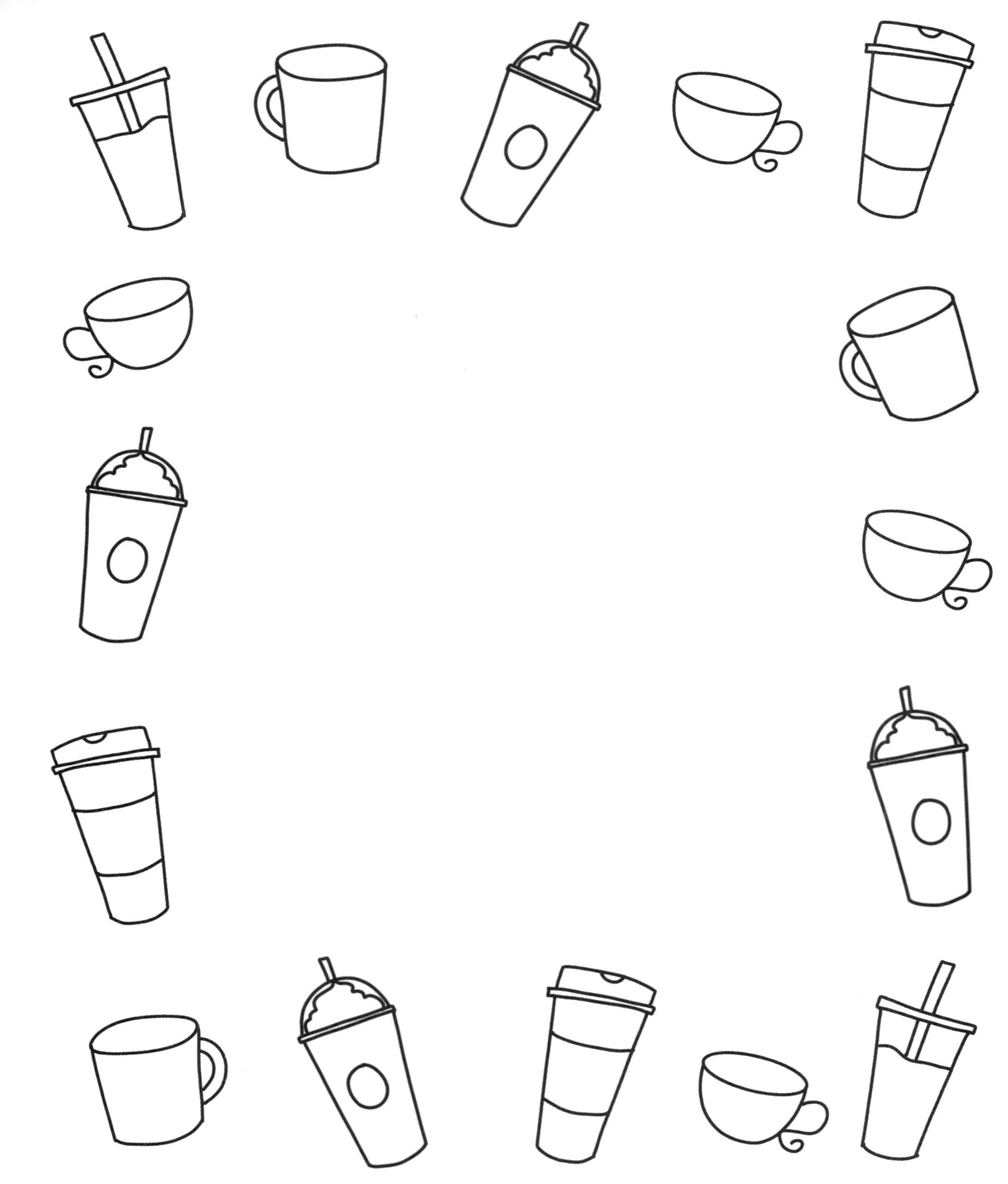

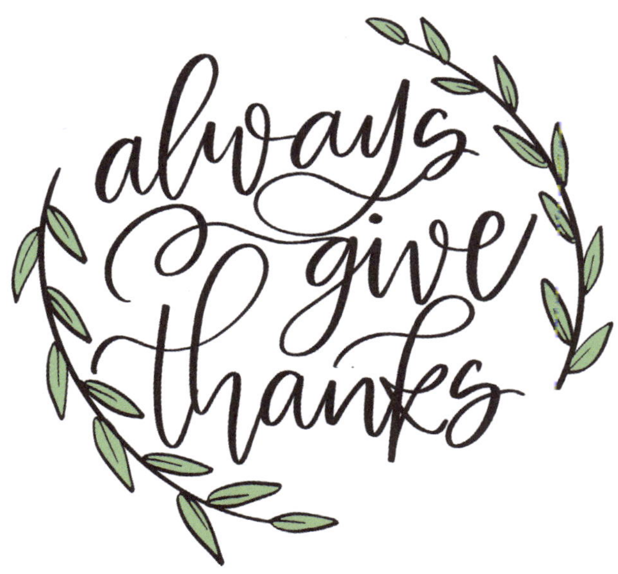

Let's try another round design, this time with three words and a different border. We'll be lettering the phrase "always give thanks," which is an important reminder no matter what time of year it happens to be. It's easy to get caught up in complaining about the things we think are going wrong and to take for granted all of the good things we have. But if we intentionally focus on gratitude, rather than on the negative parts of life, we'll have more joy. Certainly, this project makes a nice piece of seasonal décor around the holidays, but consider having it on display at other times, too, to help you remember to think about all the reasons you have to be grateful.

Once again, we'll start this project by sketching or tracing a circle, then positioning the phrase inside. Remember, we want to try to fill up as much of the space as possible. You'll notice that the word "give" is tucked off to the right side, which gives us some space to fill with a flourish later.

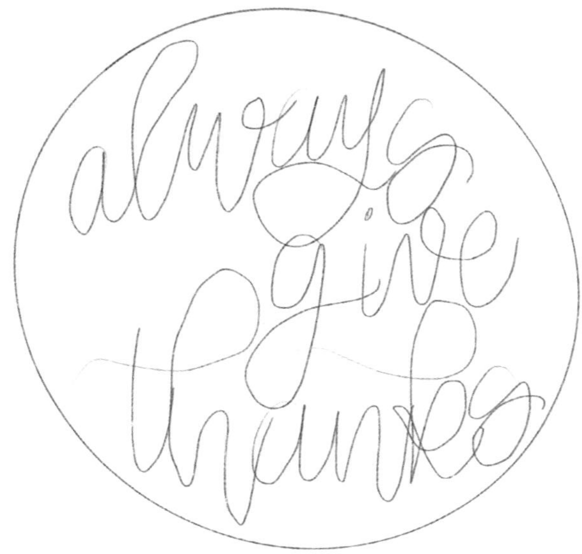

Next, letter your phrase using brush technique. I used several flourishes (page 47) to elevate the design.

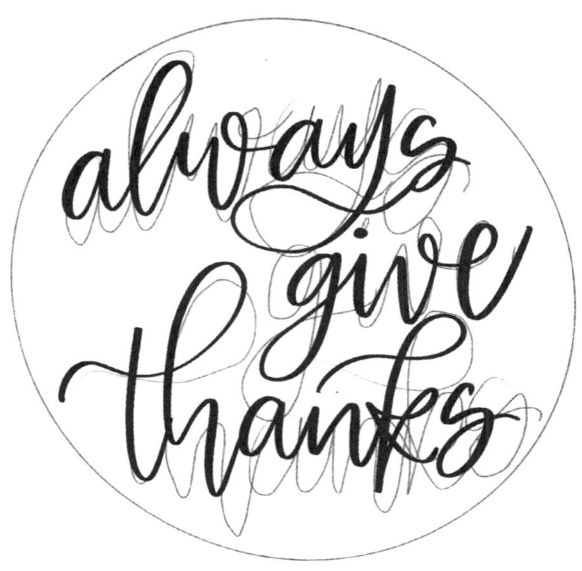

Add an extra flourish coming out from the top of the "g" and extending out to the left with a loop. Then, use your brush pen to trace around parts of the circle to create some leafy vines. Draw some pointed leaf shapes along the vines, alternating sides.

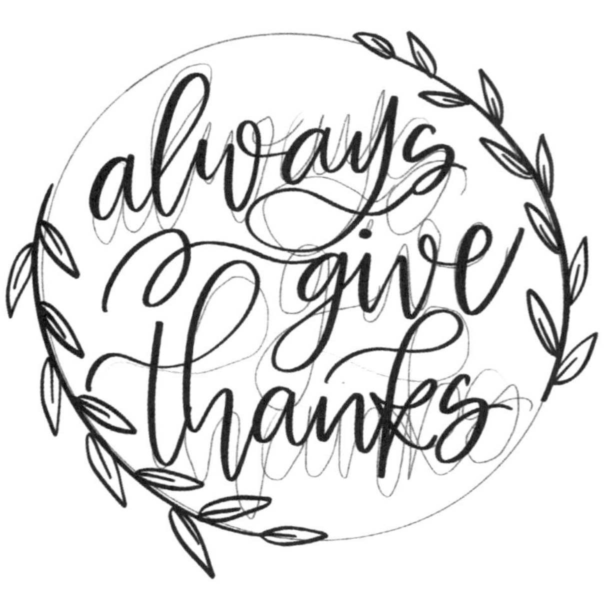

Finally, erase any remaining pencil marks to complete your design.

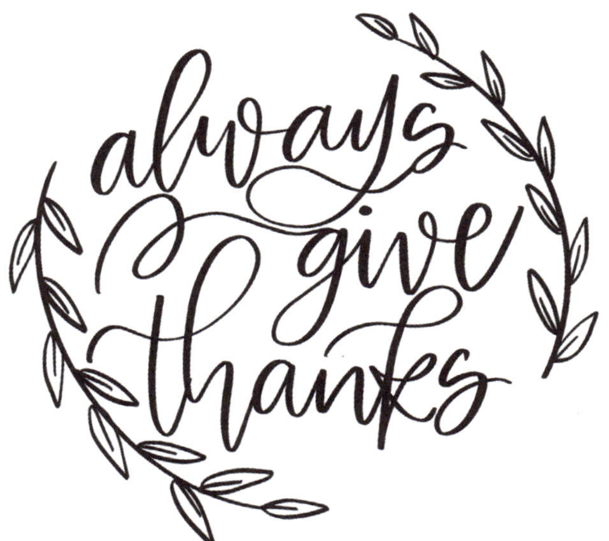

If you like, you can leave this project black and white or you can color the leaves.

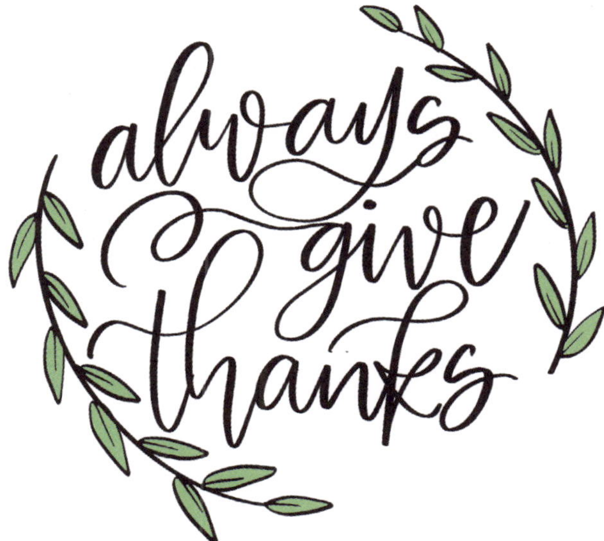

Here is a traceable version you can use as a warm-up before attempting your own project. When you're ready to try it yourself, the next page is a perfect spot for your artwork.

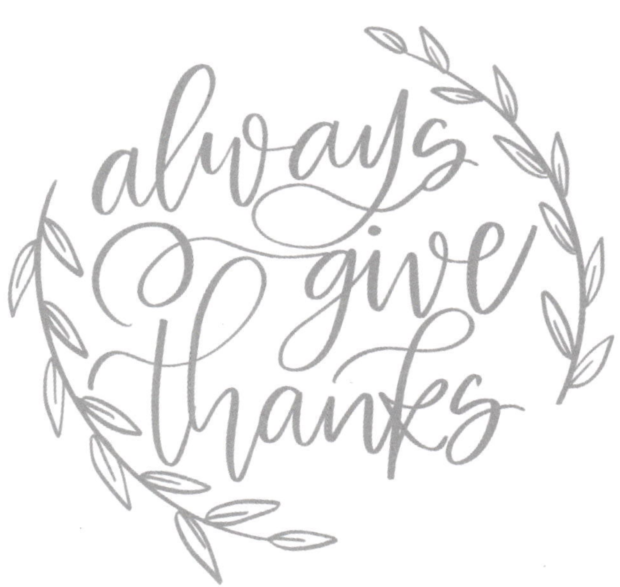

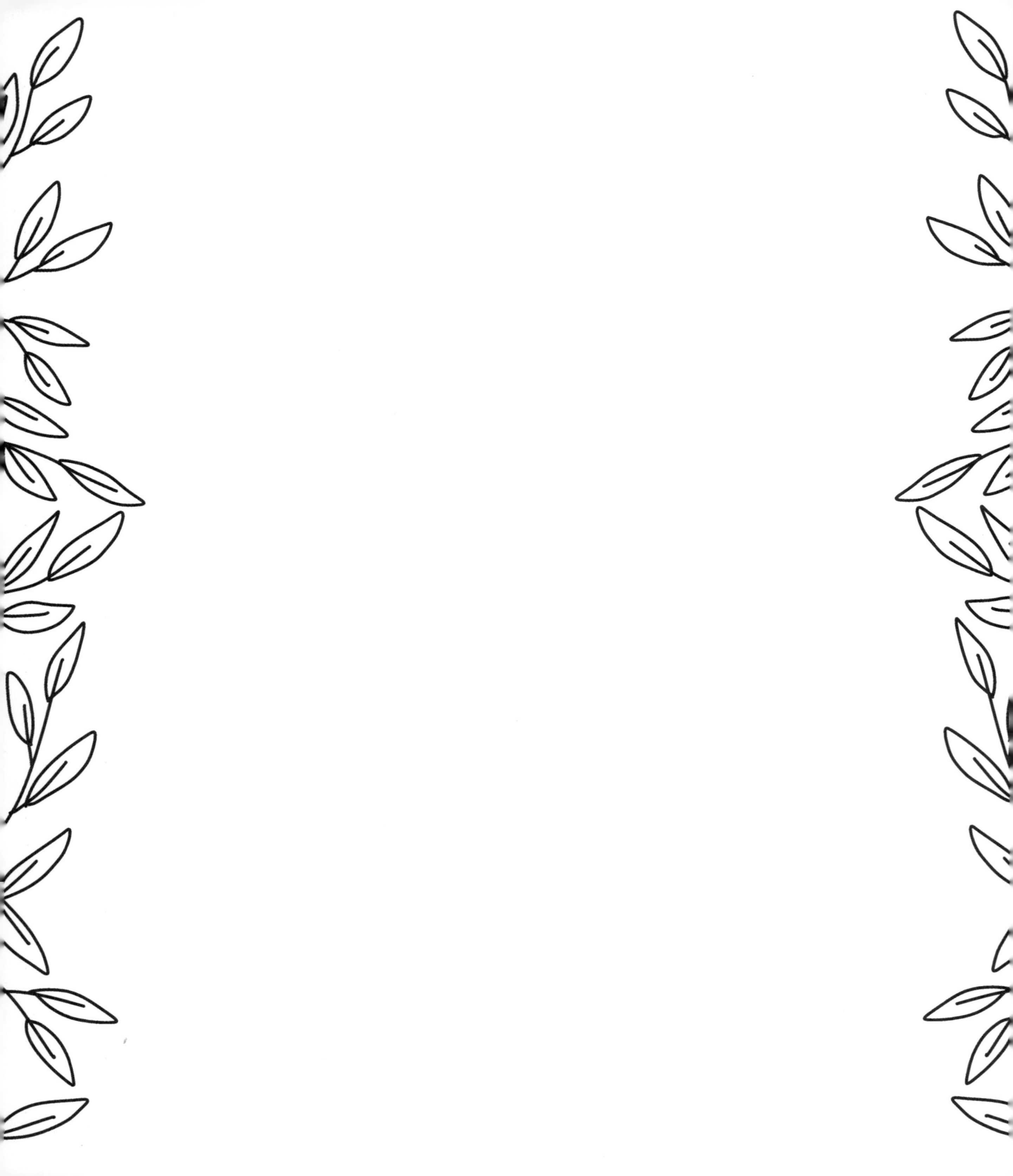

PROJECT 9

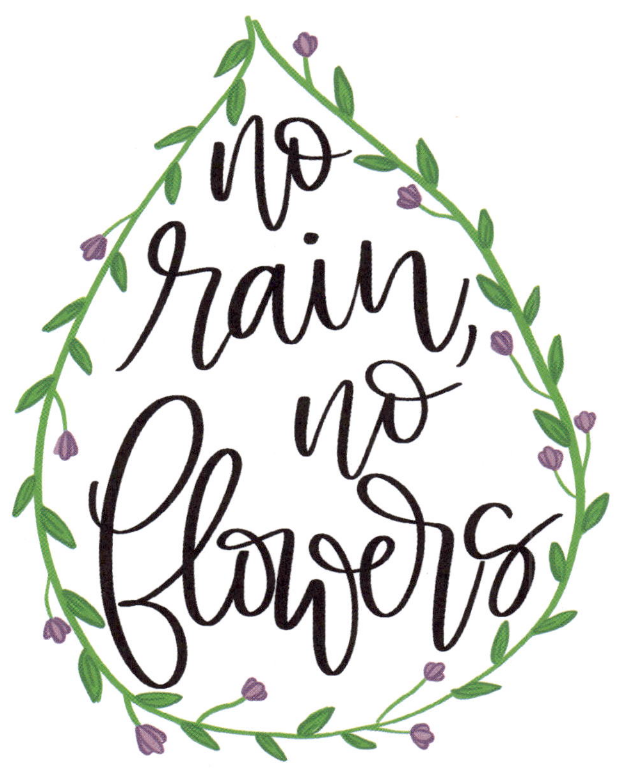

As you've seen, fitting your words inside a shape can really take a design to the next level! This time, we're going to try a new shape—a raindrop—because it fits with our quote: "no rain, no flowers." I don't know about you, but I don't typically love rainy days . . . especially since I have two dogs that dislike going outside when it's wet. But, like it or not, the rain is necessary; without it, nothing grows. If every day were pure sunshine, we wouldn't have the flowers and plants we enjoy. The same is true in life, and we grow by going through the times that are more challenging, even if they aren't fun at the time. If you know someone who is going through a tough situation, you might want to consider using this project for the front of a handmade card to encourage them! Just cut a piece of Bristol board to 4¼ x 8½ inches (10.75 x 21.5 cm), fold it in half and letter this design on the front.

Start by sketching a large teardrop shape in pencil. Don't worry if it's not perfectly symmetrical. Then, fit your script words inside.

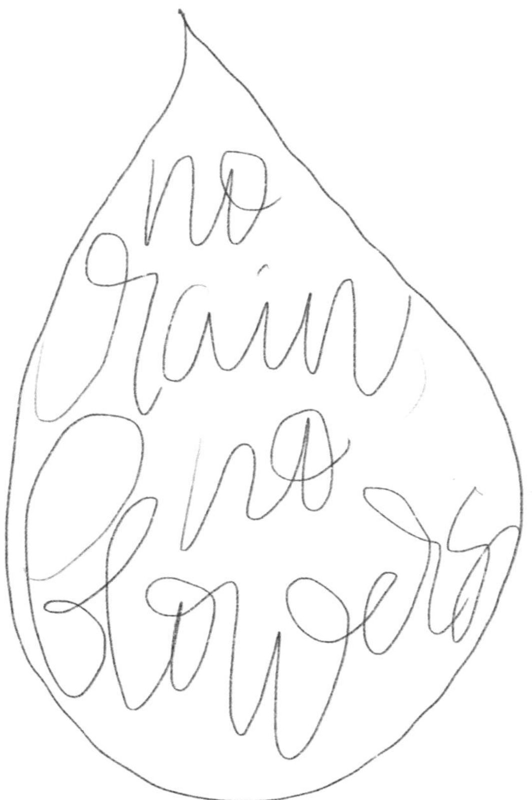

When you're satisfied with the word positions, go back over your letters with a brush pen, using that brush technique to create a contrast between thick and thin lines.

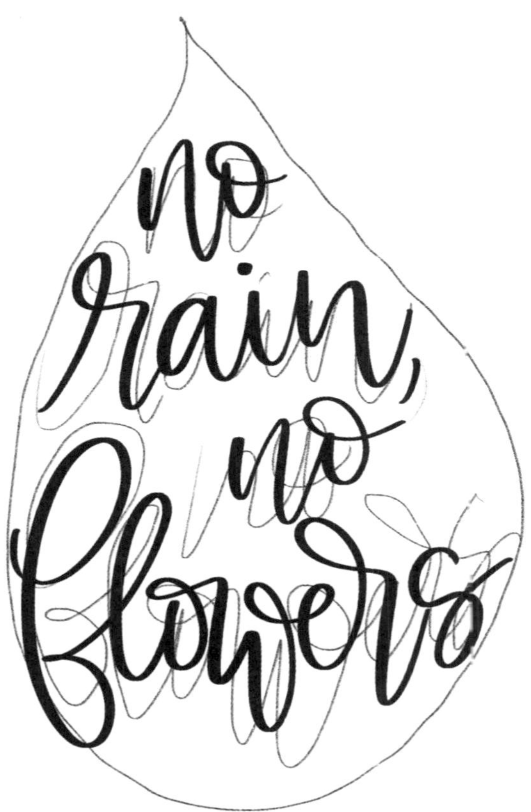

The next step is to emphasize the raindrop shape by adding a floral border. Rather than drawing in black and adding color as we did in previous projects, this time we're going to create a green vine. Choose a green marker and trace the raindrop shape with it, then add leaf shapes as well as small stems where you can draw flowers. Next, add some buds (I just created little three-petal shapes for this) in any color you like. If you prefer to draw the leaves and flowers in pencil first, feel free to do so, or you can just draw them with your markers like I did.

Erase any pencil marks you can still see and you have a beautiful finished project.

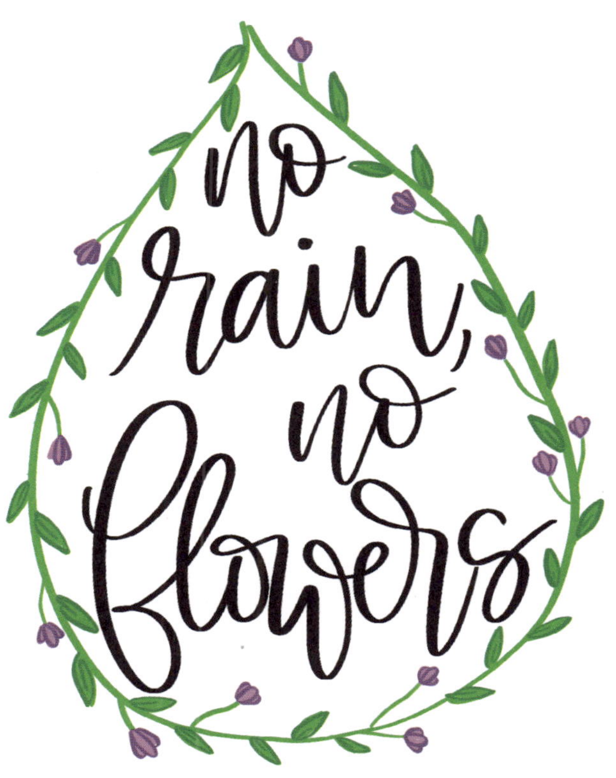

Trace the image below to get an idea of how the elements of this design work together, then try creating your own version on the page with the large floral border. Of course, you can also re-create this project on canvas, Bristol board or in your sketchbook.

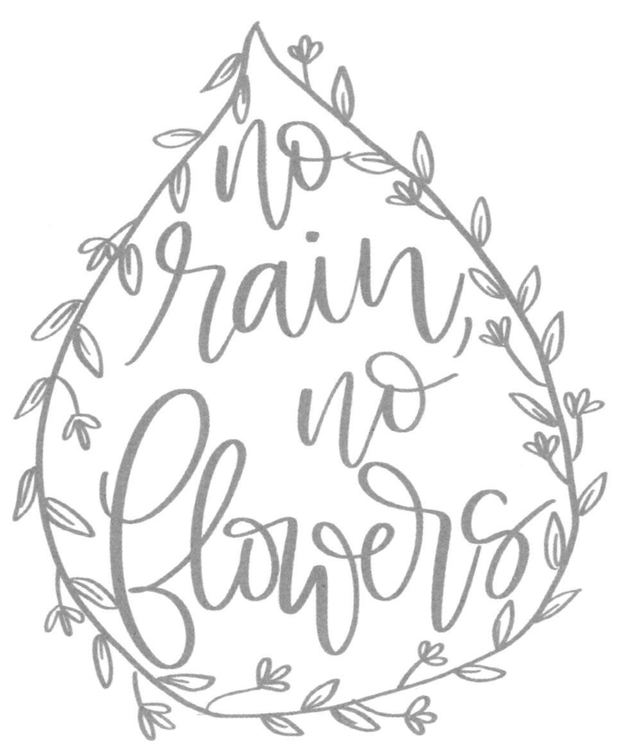

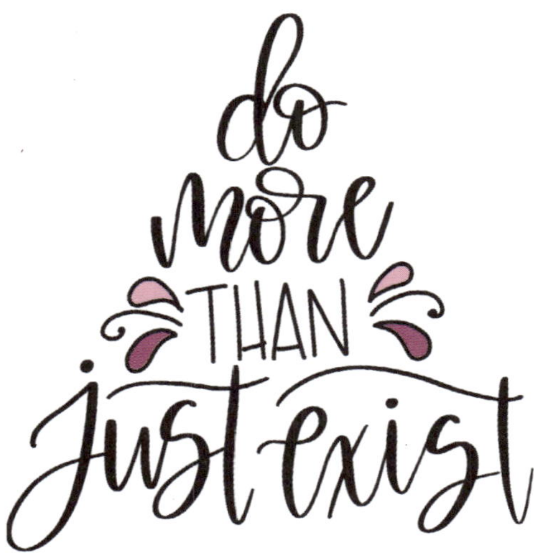

So far, we've shaped our designs into a house, a circle and a raindrop. Let's push ourselves with this next project and create a triangle shape with our phrase! I chose the quote "do more THAN just exist" for two reasons. One is that it's a wonderful reminder that we only get one life and it's up to us to make it count. We can choose just to go through the motions and exist or we can choose to really live life to the fullest. This message challenges me to think about the impact I want to make in the lives of others and to take advantage of every opportunity that comes my way. The other reason it's perfect for this project is that the phrase naturally breaks itself into sections that get longer as the quote goes on, making it easy to shape into our triangle!

Start by using a pencil to sketch a rough triangle, then position your words inside. Remember, we want to fill up as much of the center space as possible, so it's the perfect time to use all of the kinds of bounce (page 75), as well as some fun flourishes (page 47) to help us do just that.

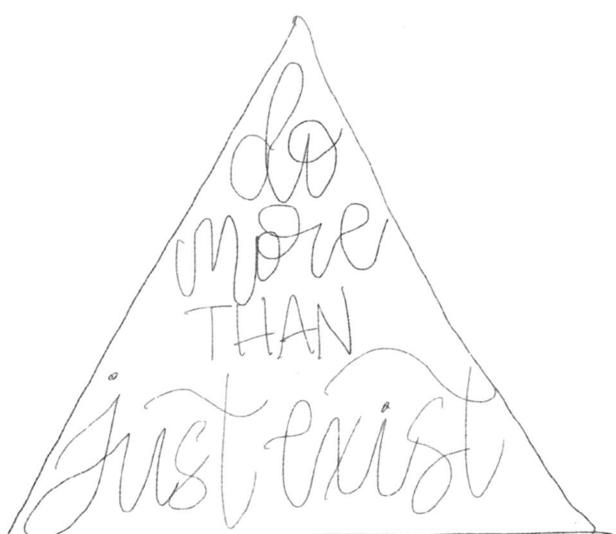

Next, use a brush pen to letter "do more" and "just exist." The same rules about when to apply pressure to the pen tip work for flourishes, too. Whenever your pen is moving in a downward motion, you'll want to press. Then, use a fine-tip drawing pen to print the word "than." We have some extra space on the left and right of that word, so let's fill it in with a few little sideways teardrop shapes and swirls.

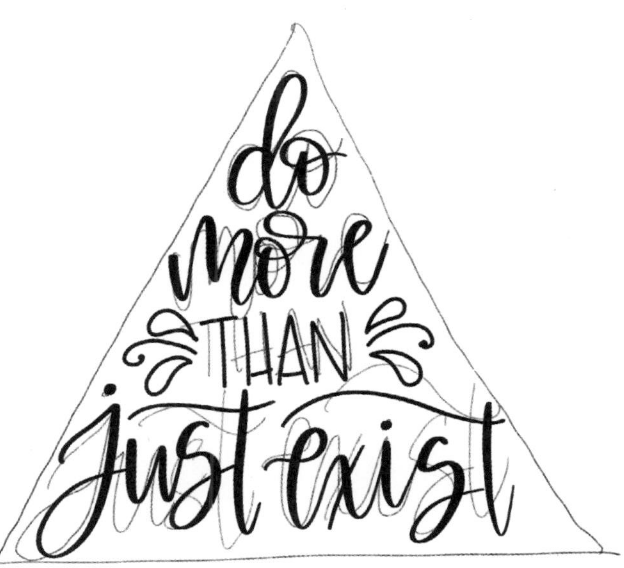

Erase your pencil lines, then color the teardrops to make the embellishments pop. Rather than adding a border around the triangle, we're going to let the lettering itself show off the shaping.

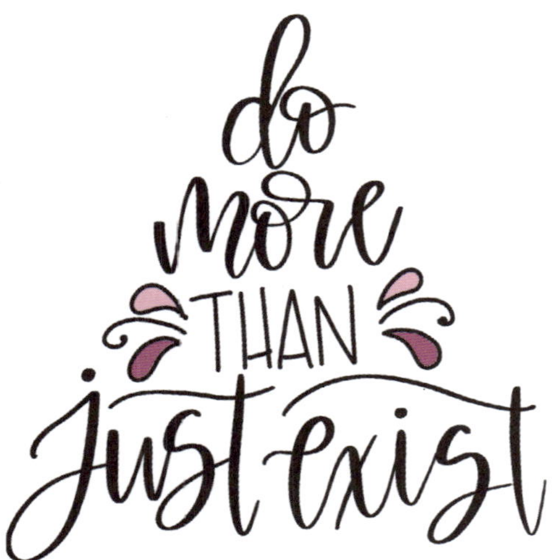

Ready to give it a go? Trace the image below to get a sense for the flourishes I used and how they help fill the space inside the triangle. Notice how the ascender of the "d" gives the triangle its tip and the way I crossed my "t"s helps fill in white space between the lines. Then, it's time for you to make your own masterpiece on the next page.

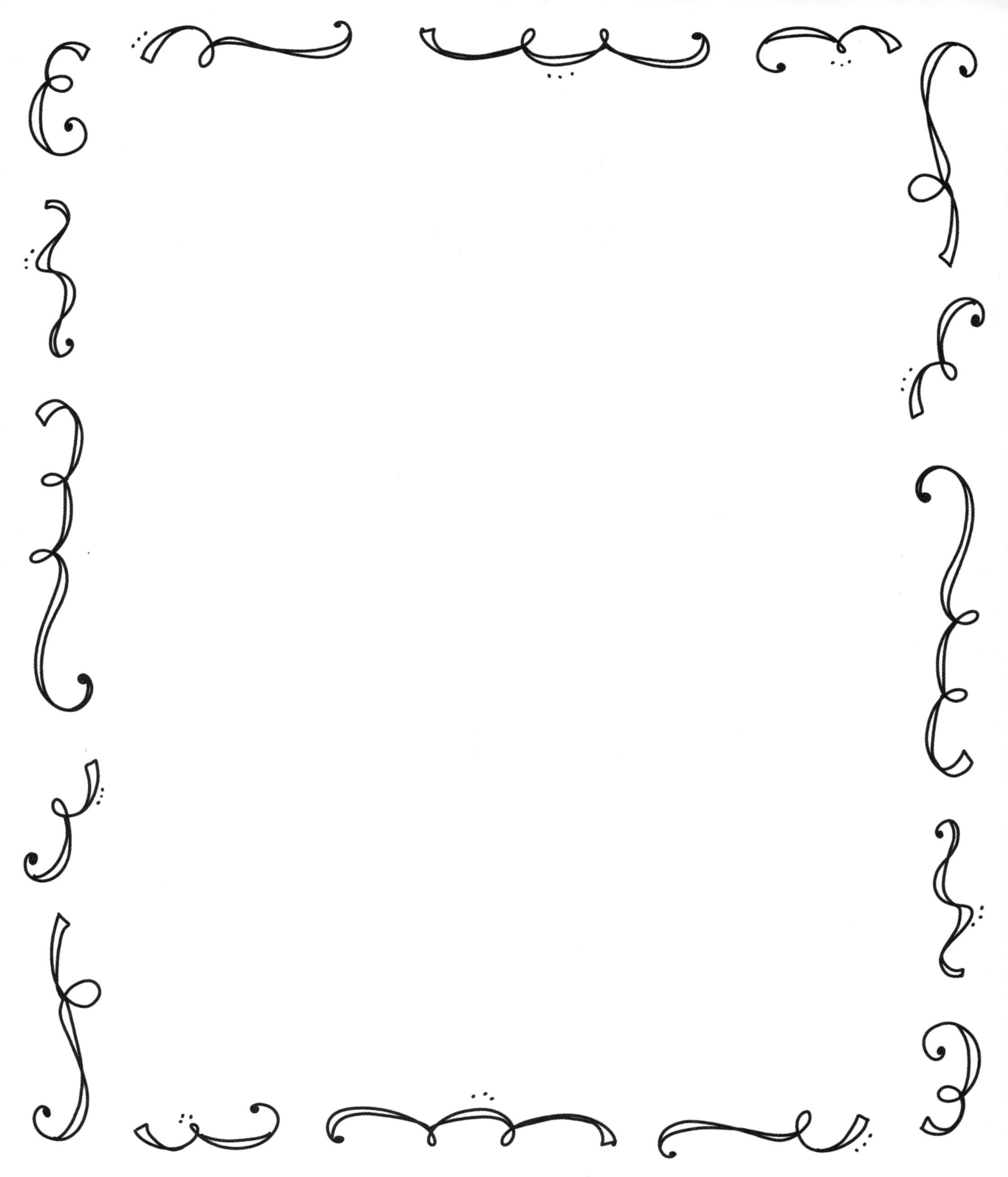

PROJECT 11

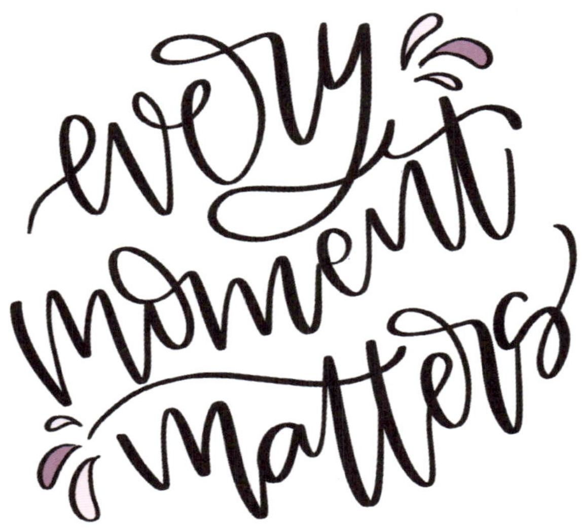

Our next design is based on a circle again, but like we did in the previous project, we're going to let the lettering itself suggest the shape rather than actually drawing or tracing a round border. We'll be lettering the quote "every moment matters," which is something I try to remind myself as I get caught up in the daily grind. The things we do can feel monotonous sometimes (I get awfully tired of unloading the dishwasher every morning), but the reality is that every moment of our life holds potential. Even in the midst of the mundane, we can come up with a great idea. In the middle of something uninspiring, we can find a moment of connection with someone we love. Every breath, every moment holds possibility. Perhaps I should display my project with this quote above the dishwasher. Where will you display yours?

To begin, sketch/trace a circle, then fill in the words "every moment matters." I positioned my words on an angle and made use of lots of bounce to make sure the whole circle was filled (see page 75 for details on bounce technique). Remember, we can tilt our letters and also use downstroke drift, which allows us to place each letter exactly where we want it to go. The goal is to fill up as much of the white space in the circle as possible, so we want to try to position our letters like puzzle pieces that fit together line by line.

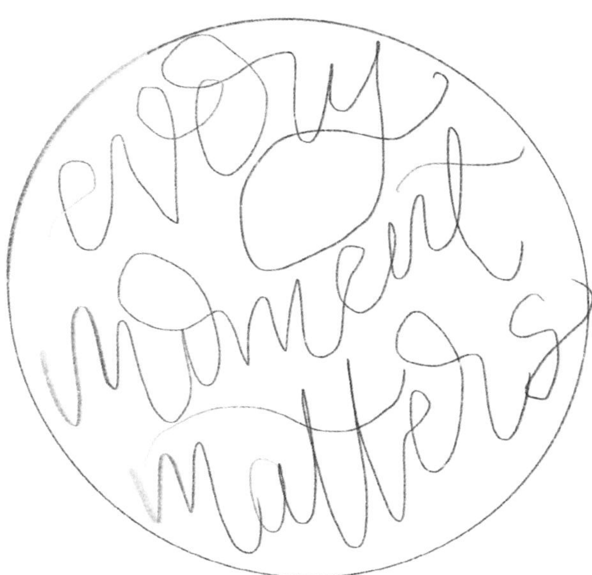

Now, it's brush pen time. Letter your words, making sure to pay attention to the direction your pen is moving at all times.

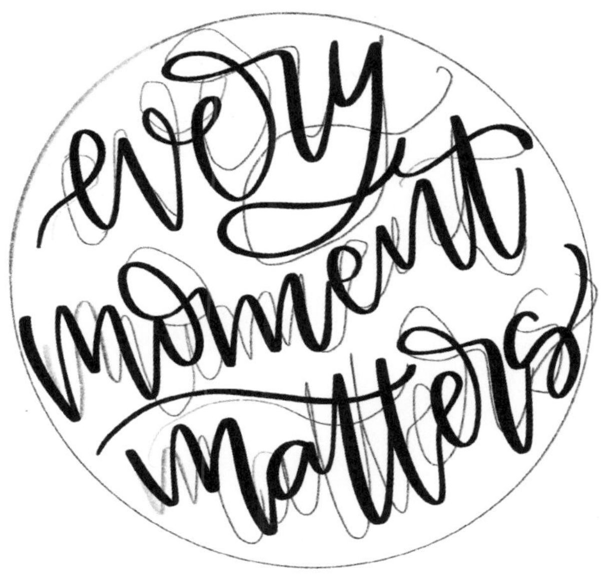

Draw a few curving sideways teardrop shapes to fill in those last little open spaces and suggest the circular shape. Erase any pencil lines you can still see from the circle itself, as well as the words.

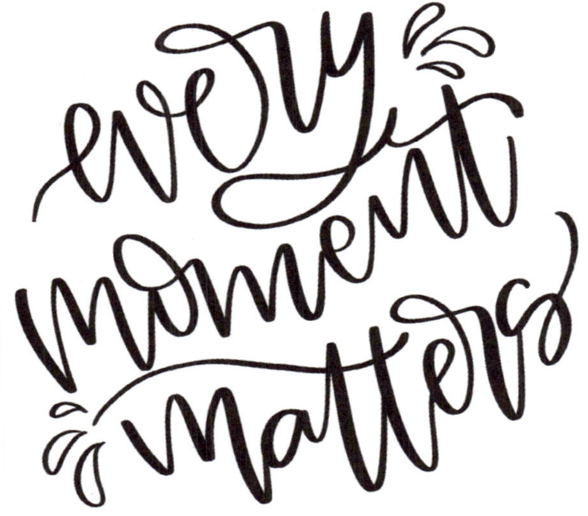

Finish your project by coloring the teardrop shapes any shade you like.

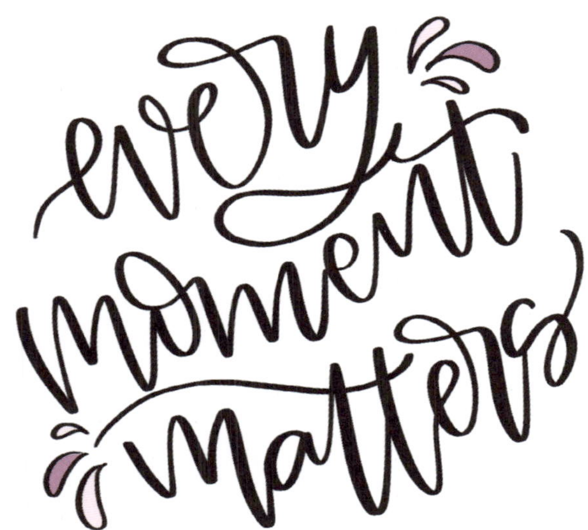

Here's a copy of my design that you can trace to get a little bit of practice and see how I used bounce to my advantage filling the circle. Then, try it for yourself on the next page. The circular border reinforces the shape (and helps you keep on track).

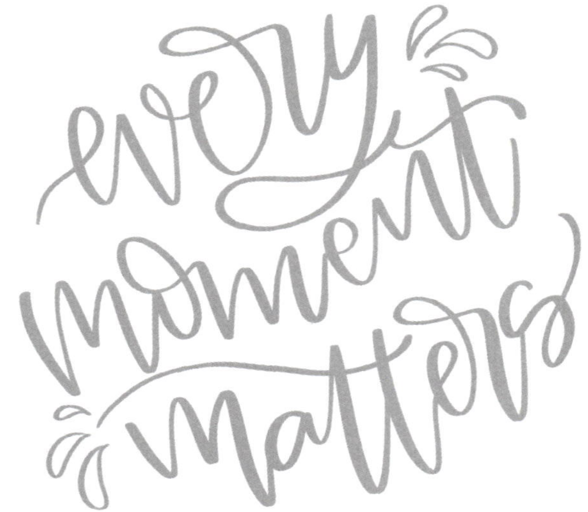

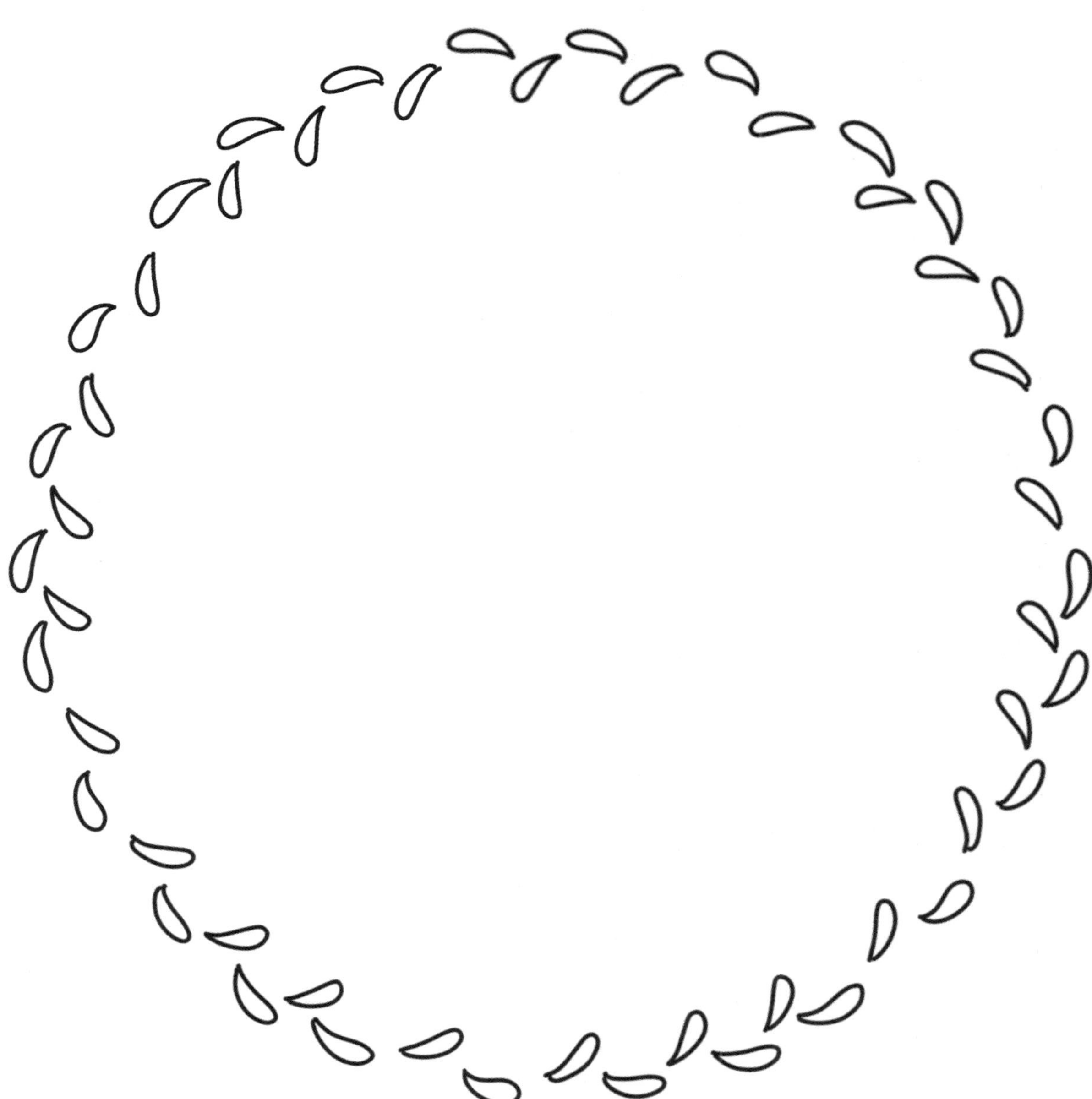

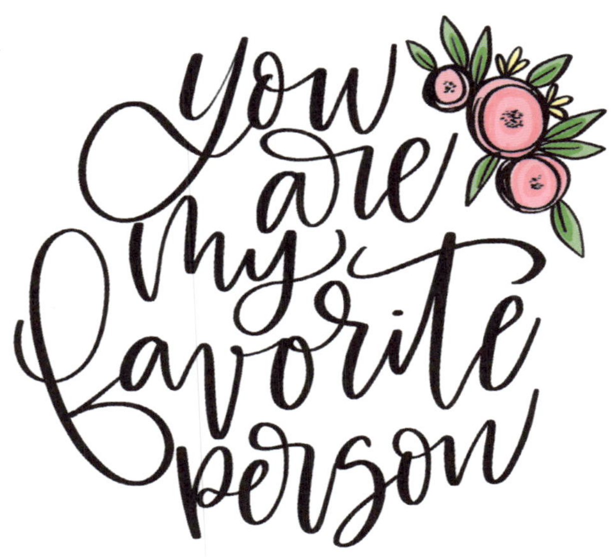

Before we move on from round designs, let's add one more type of embellishment to the mix: florals! We are also going to challenge ourselves by trying this technique with a slightly longer phrase.

To create this project, sketch or trace a circle in pencil that's large enough to fit the quote "you are my favorite person." Pencil in the placement of your words, all in script. Don't forget to use bounce and flourishing (pages 75 and 47) to make your words take up as much of the open space as possible.

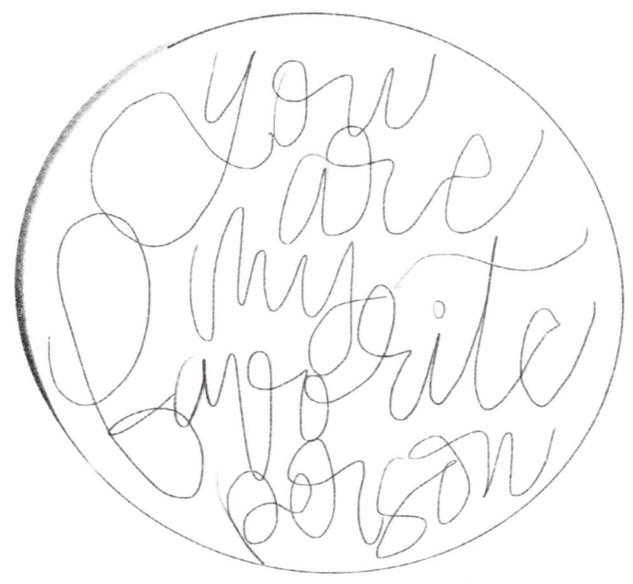

Use your brush pen to brush letter the phrase, making sure to apply pressure on all the downstrokes so you get the beautiful contrast between thick and thin lines in every letter.

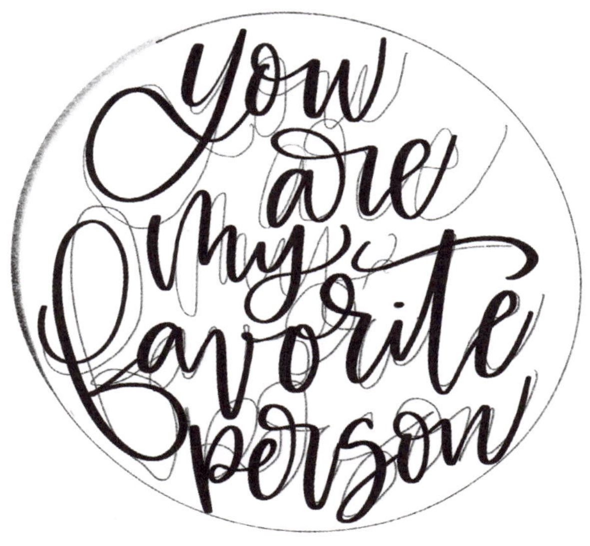

Erase your pencil lines. Then, in the top right area of the quote, add a floral doodle. The larger flowers are what I call "messy circle" blooms. Just draw a circle shape and trace it a few times, then add dots in the center. I grouped three of these together, with the largest one in the center. Then, add leaf shapes and a few little petaled flowers made up of three upside down teardrops.

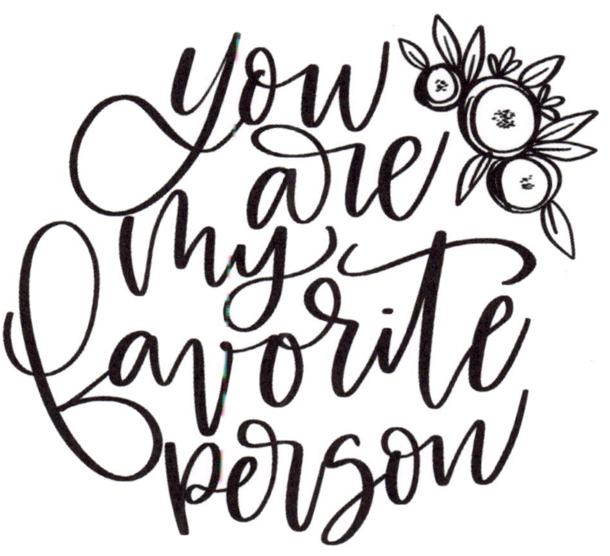

Finally, color your flowers and leaves to complete the project. This would make a beautiful greeting card for a special person, don't you think?

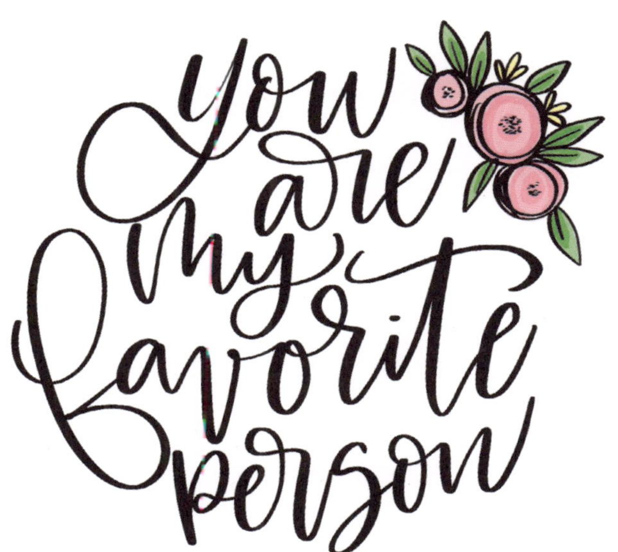

You can practice both the lettering and the doodles by tracing the image below, then create your own unique version on the next page. Of course, you can also create more masterpieces on other surfaces, too, so that you can share your creation with that special someone.

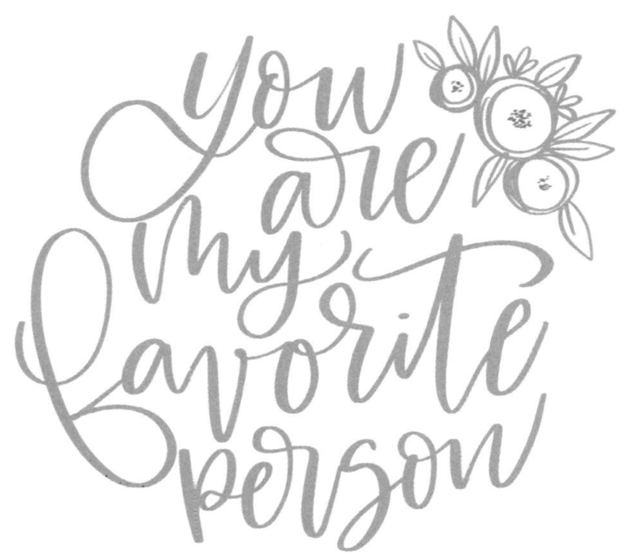

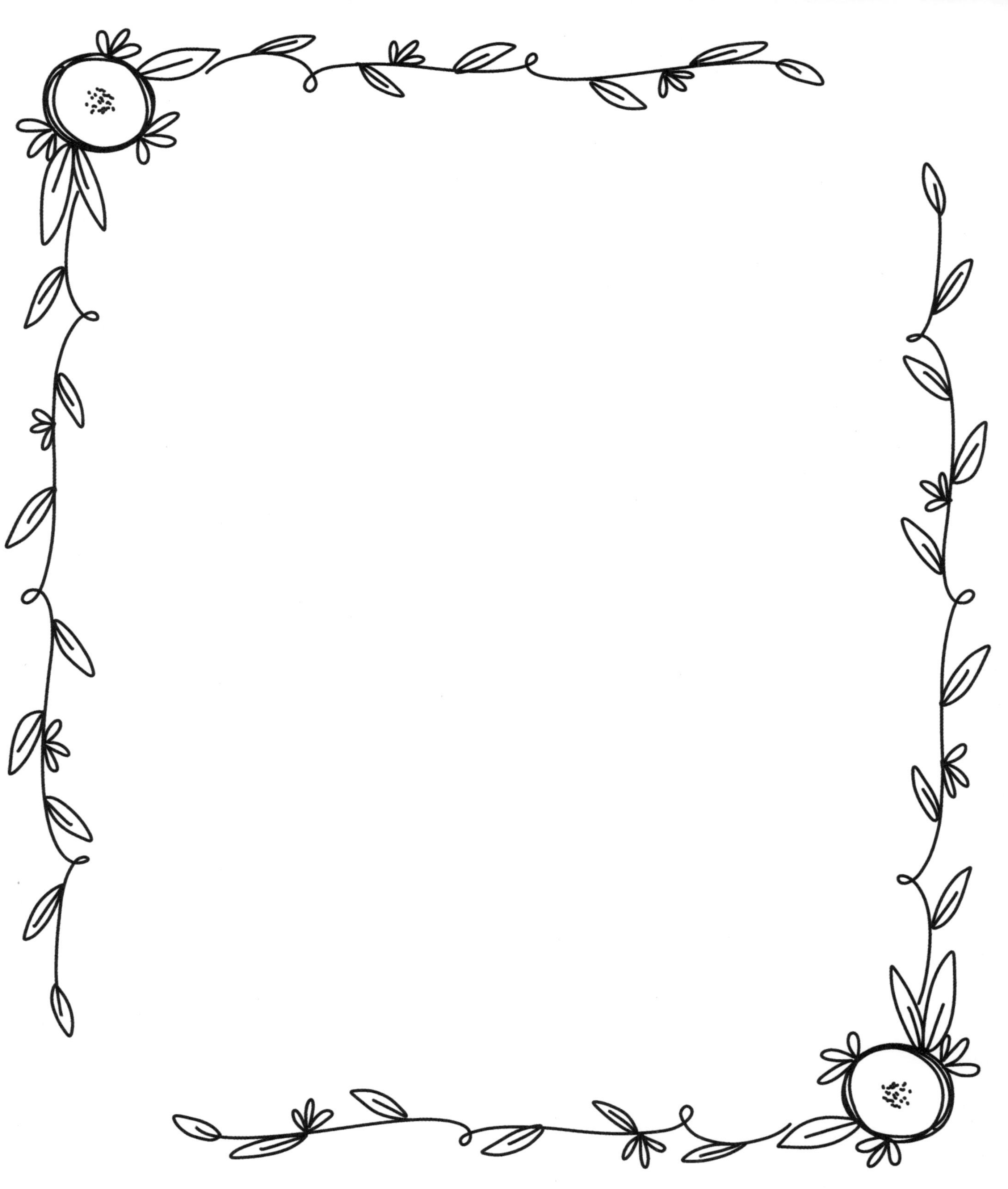

PROJECT 13

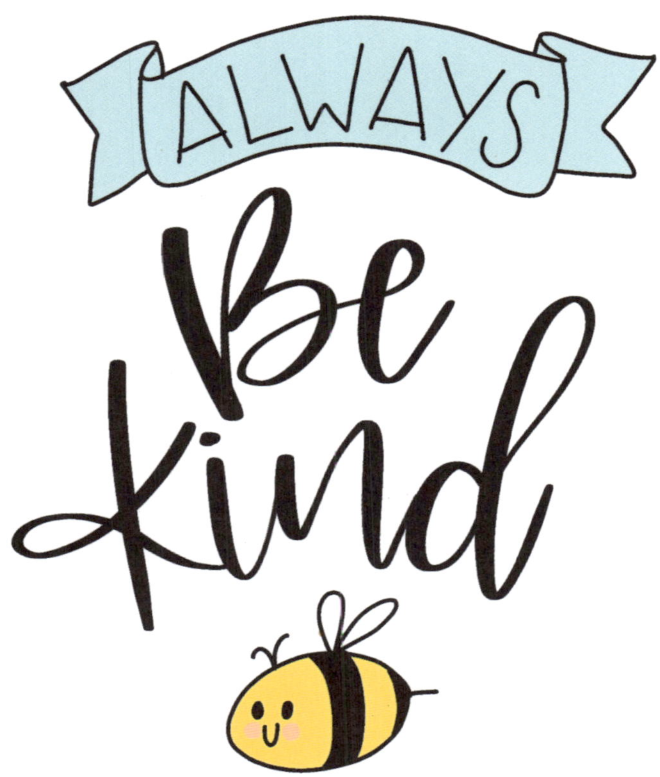

For our next project, we're going to incorporate both a banner and a fun doodle to really make this quote pop. Banners are wonderful design elements because they give us a fun way to contain some of the less important words in a phrase. For this project, we're going to use a banner to frame the printed word "ALWAYS," then brush letter "Be kind" in large brush script. To make it extra fun, we're going to add a little bee doodle at the bottom of the design. After all, what could "bee" better than being kind to everyone always? It sure makes the world a better place!

The first step is to use a pencil to lightly sketch the banner (see page 89 for a tutorial on drawing a banner), words and bee shape. The bee is simply an oval with two teardrops for wings, along with stripes, a face, a little pair of antennae and a stinger.

Next, use a brush pen to brush letter "Be kind." Then, use a fine-tip black drawing marker to create the banner, the bee and the final word.

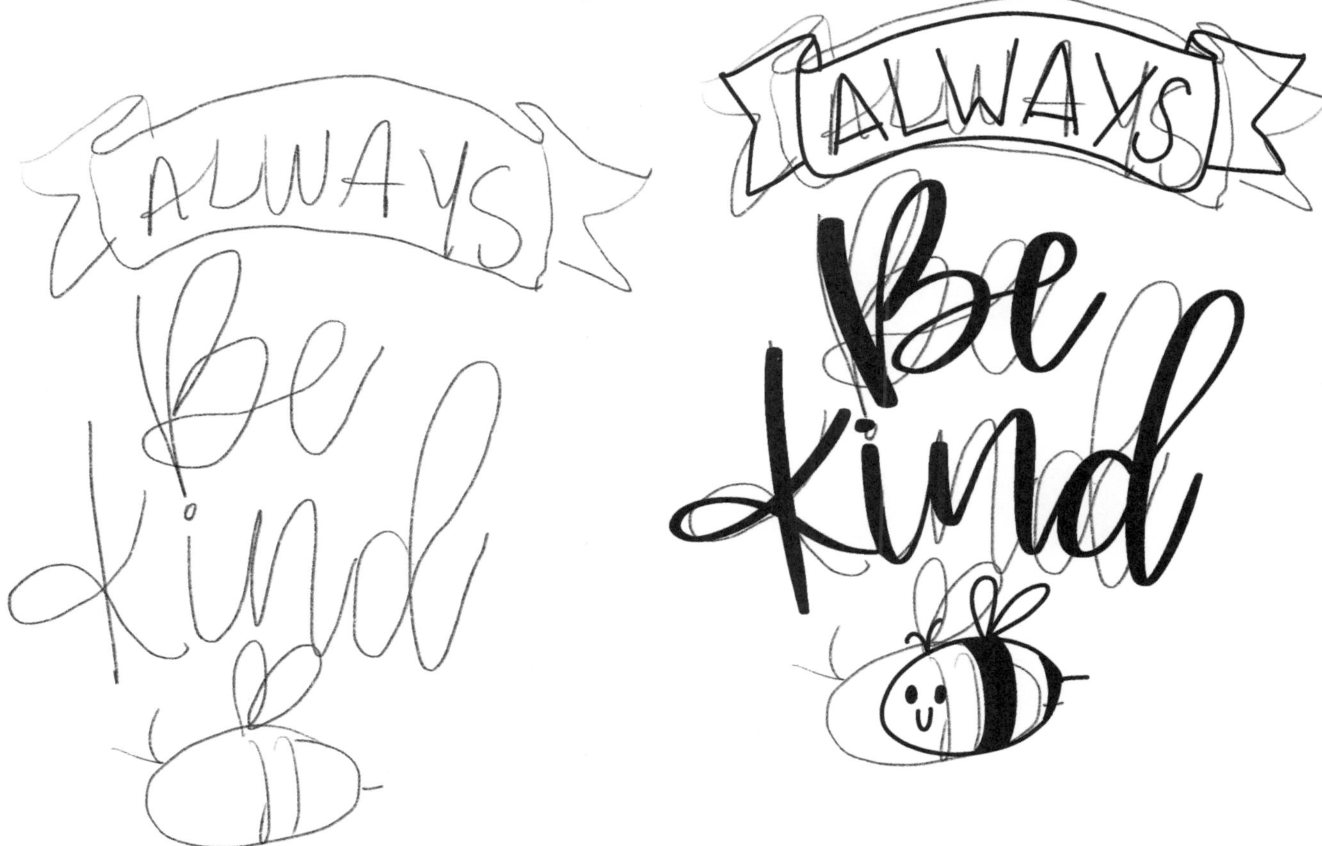

Erase your remaining pencil marks, then color the banner and the bee. This project would be adorable as a lunch box note or even as a sign for a bedroom or locker.

To get your lettering hand warmed up, take a minute to trace the copy of my design found below. This will give you a chance to practice forming the banner shape, as well as the cute little bee. Then, try your own version on the page with the beehive illustration!

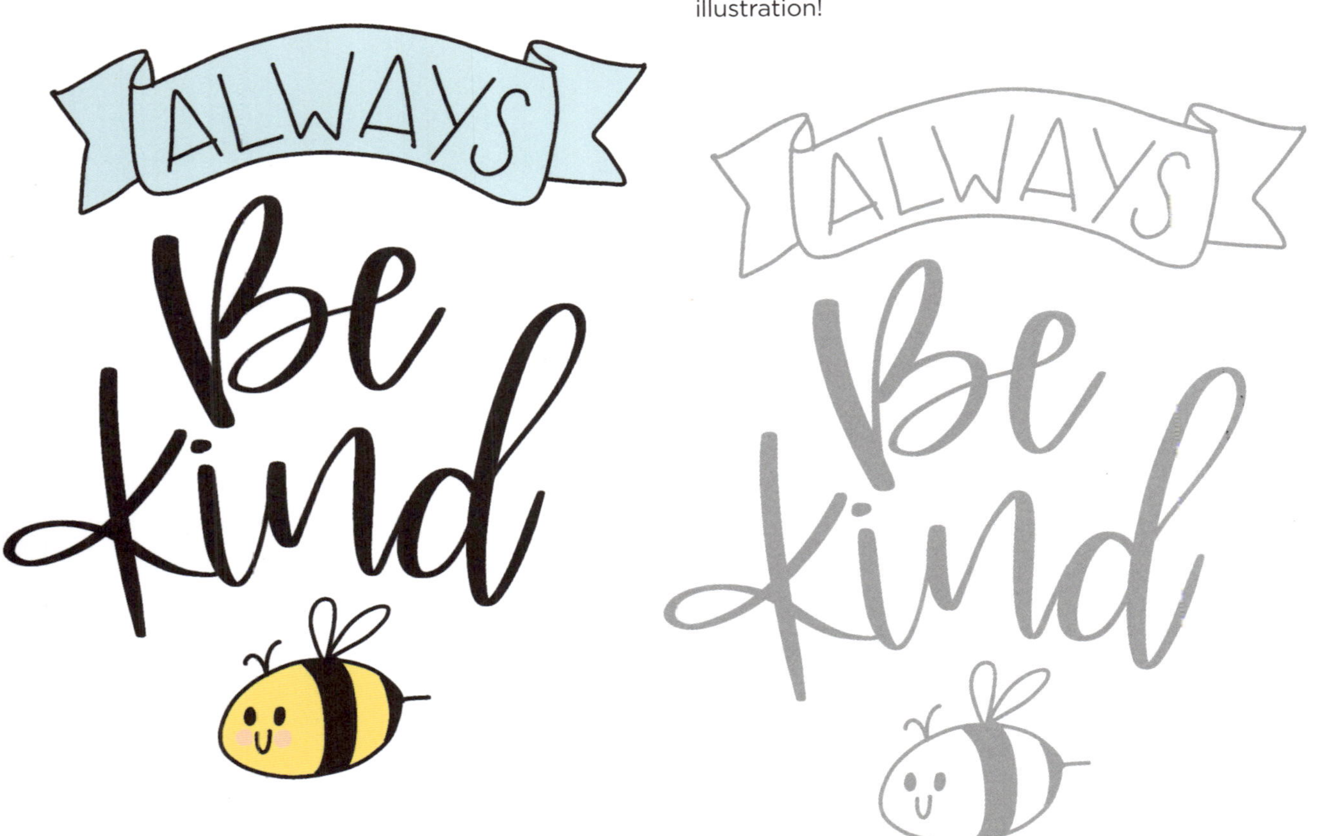

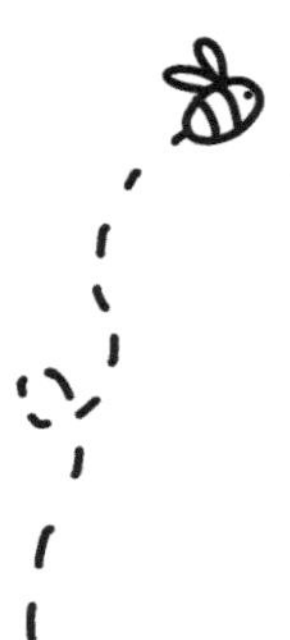

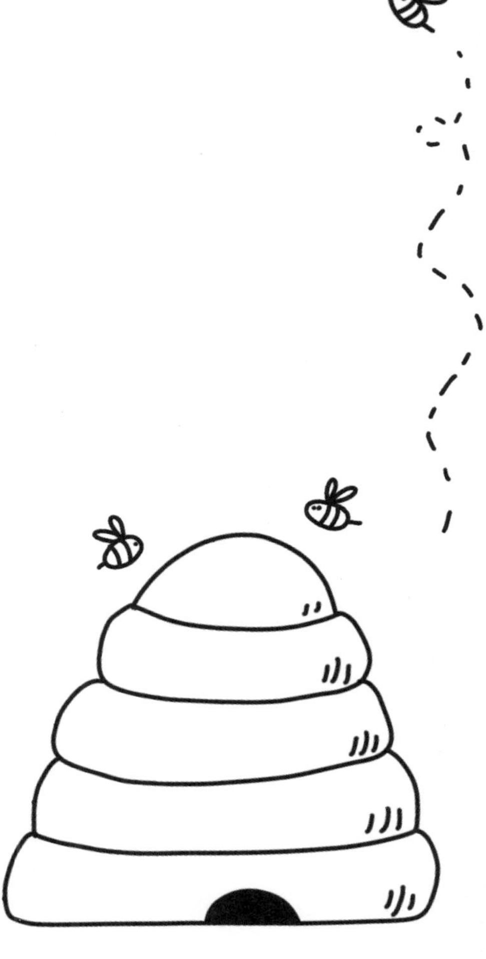

PROJECT 14

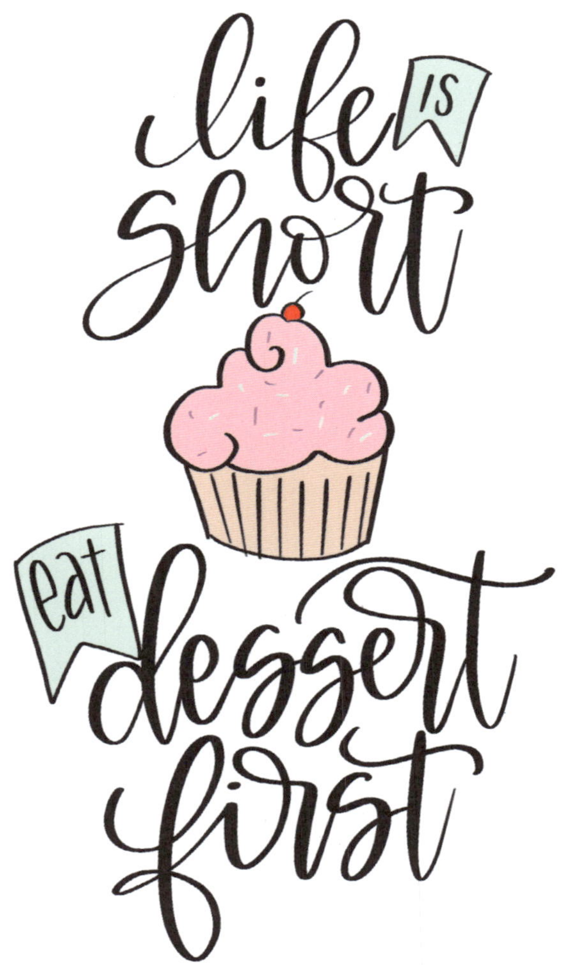

The next project we're going to tackle contains some important advice: "Life is short, eat dessert first." As a huge fan of ice cream, cookies, pie and just about all sweet things, this is the kind of mantra I can fully support! It's also an adorable project to display in the kitchen. Just like the little bee in our previous project, we'll see that a well-placed doodle can really bring a hand-lettered phrase to life. Since we're talking about eating dessert first, a cupcake doodle is the perfect accent this time. We're also going to use a few tiny banners for the little words "IS" and "eat."

The first step for this project is to lightly sketch the words, the banner and the cupcake shape as shown below. The banners are simply the letter "w" with a line across the top and the cupcake is a series of swirls on top of a rounded rectangle base. I placed the cupcake in the center of the two halves of the phrase to help emphasize the punch line.

Once you are happy with your basic sketch, let's make it permanent. Brush letter your script words using a brush pen. Then, use either a brush pen or a drawing marker to trace the rest of the words and images.

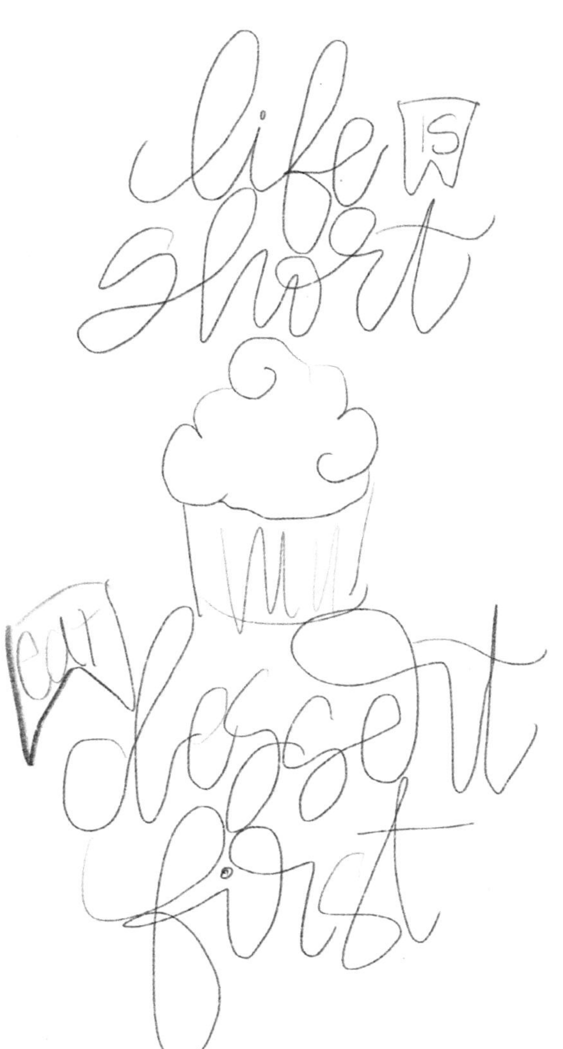

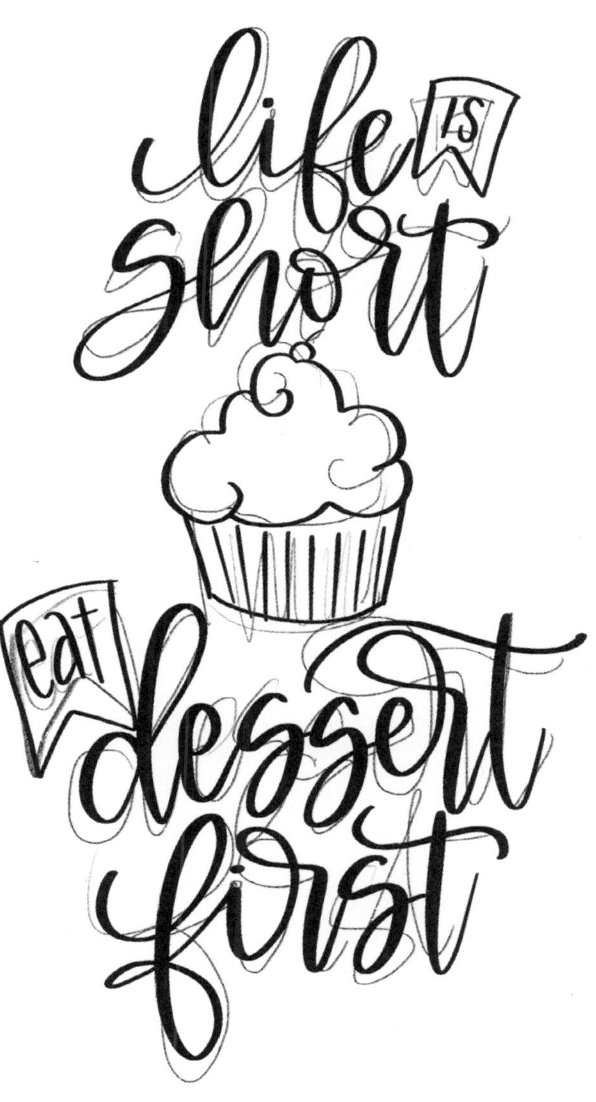

Erase your pencil lines, then add color to the banners and the cupcake doodle. Feel free to add sprinkles and any other decorations you like.

To get some practice with these new doodles, you can trace my design below. Then, give it a try on your own, either on the provided page and/or on a canvas to hang in your kitchen!

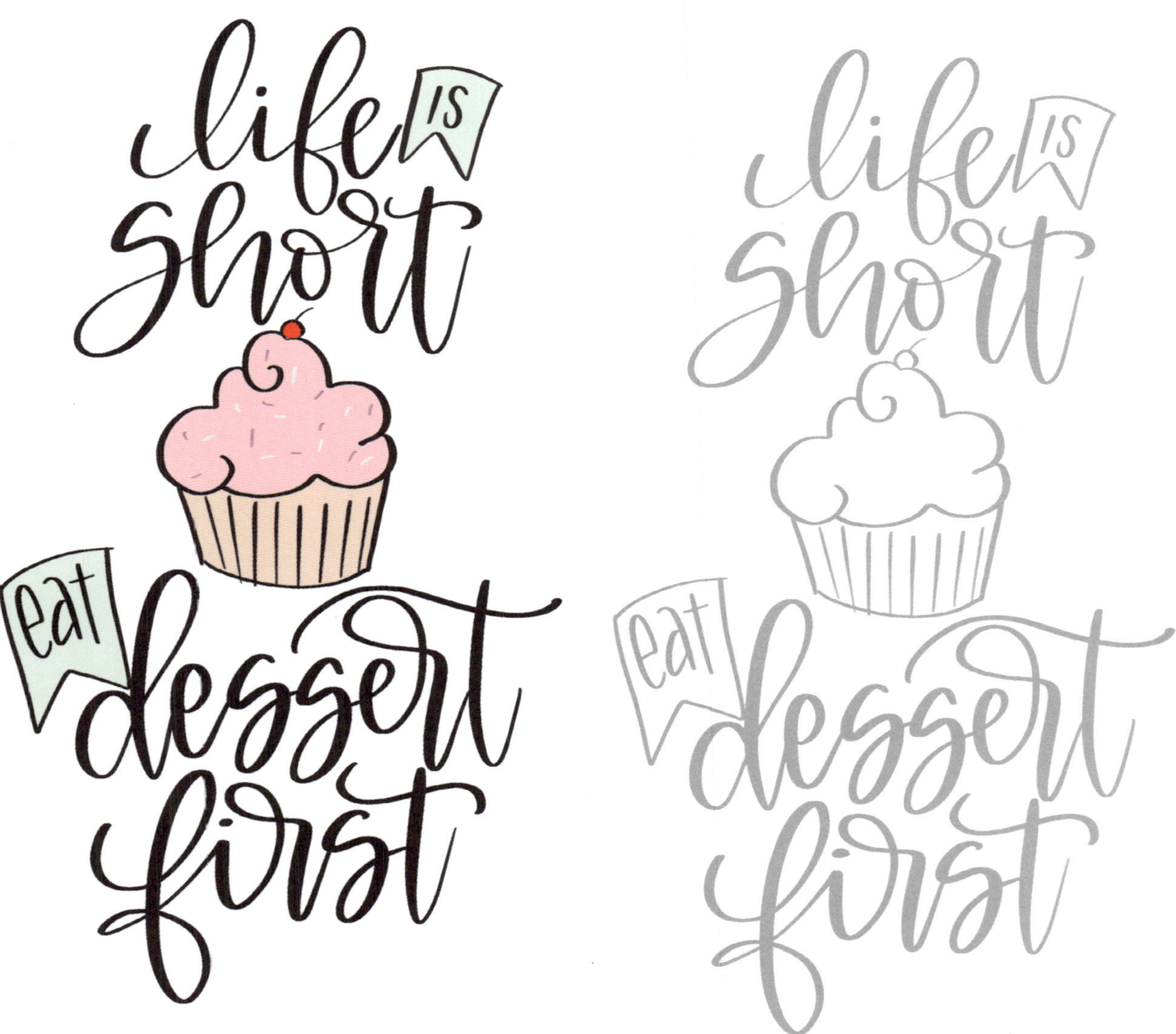

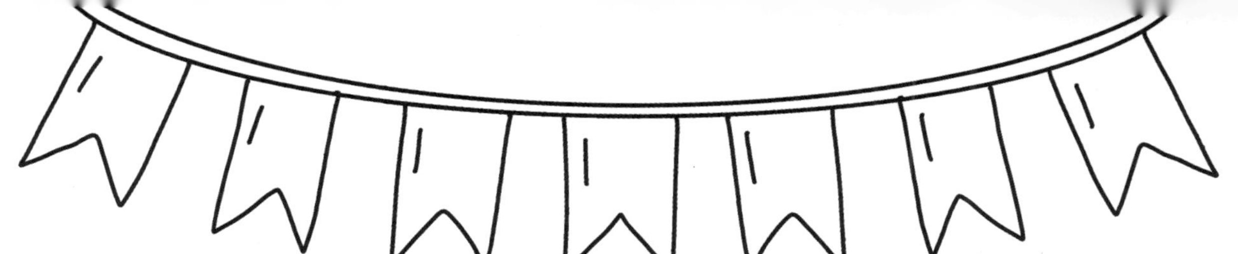

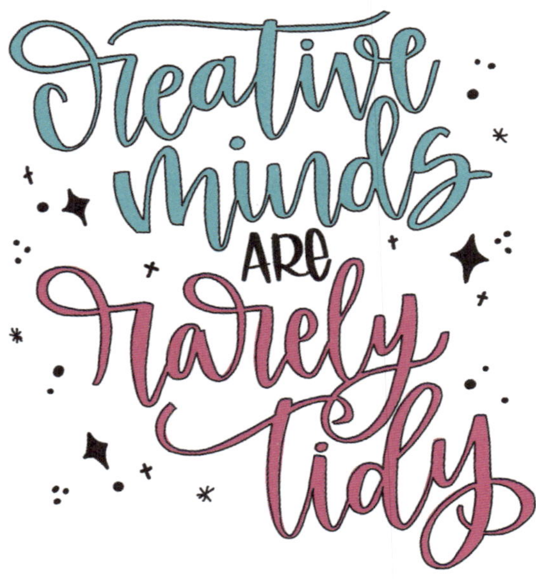

I don't know about you, but I fully relate to the idea that creative minds are rarely tidy. Just ask my husband or take a tour of my crafting space when I'm mid-project and you'll see just what I mean. Those of us with an artistic bent often tend to be less organized than some of our more analytical friends . . . and that's okay! It means we can push the limits and think outside of the box. In fact, sometimes our lettered designs can take on unusual shapes. Rather than a simple circle, triangle or other basic shape for this project, we're going to attempt something a little different. This shape is like a lightning bolt: a tilted rectangle on top of a second tilted rectangle that goes out to the left.

To get started, use your pencil to sketch a shape similar to the one shown below and position the words inside.

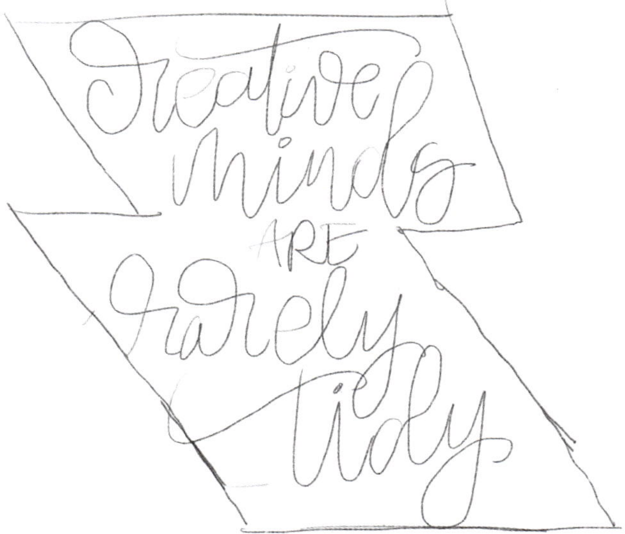

We are going to use the outline technique for this phrase, so choose two of your favorite colored brush pens with medium to large tips. Use one to letter the words "creative minds" and the other for the words "rarely tidy." Use a third color or a black marker to print "ARE" in between the two.

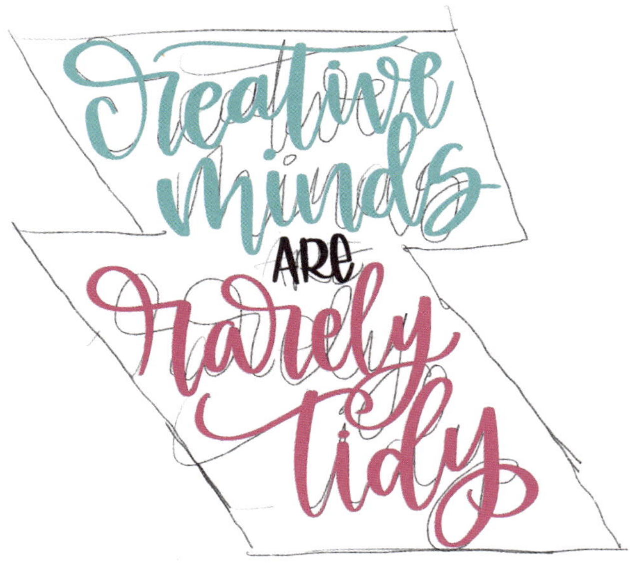

Erase your pencil lines, then outline your lettering with a fine-tip black marker (see page 73 for details on outline technique). Finally, use that fine-tip marker to add some simple embellishments—diamonds, dots and asterisks—in the open space around your words.

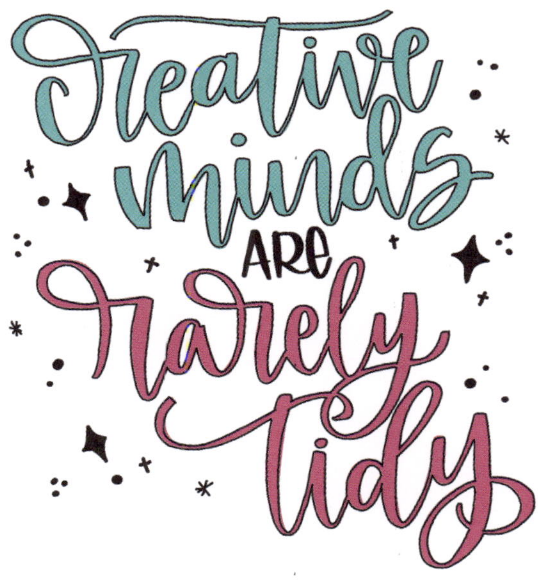

As always, you can use the traceable image below to practice the shape, the lettering and the embellishments before trying the design on your own. Then, create your own masterpiece on the bordered page.

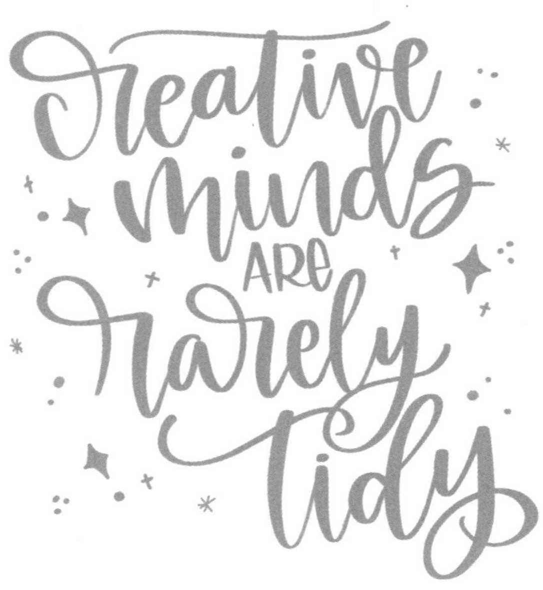

PROJECT 16

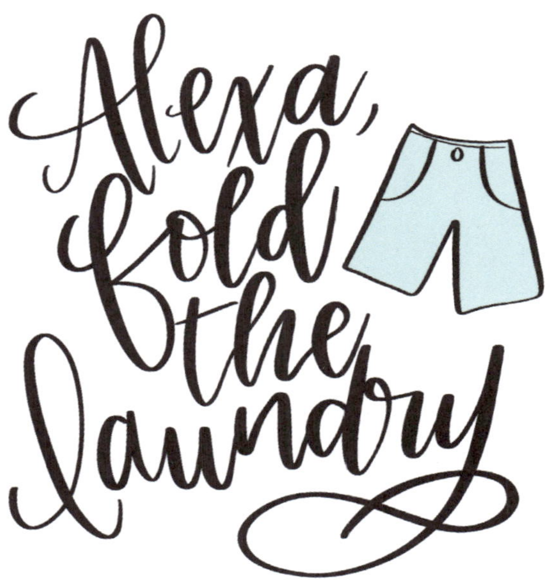

When it comes to creating a design layout, we've looked at lettering on several straight(ish) lines and lettering inside a shape. This next project will allow us to try something new: fitting our words together like puzzle pieces. To do this, we take into account the ascenders and descenders in our words and create a layout that lets them work together to create a compact design. We're going to try this using the phrase "Alexa, fold the laundry." Although I don't personally have a robot assistant, I can definitely relate to the wish that someone else would do my least favorite chores for me! I mean, why does laundry never ever end? Just when I think I'm finished, I look around and my family has the nerve to be wearing clothes and making them dirty! Someone send help! This project is a perfect choice for a sign on the laundry room door, don't you think?

We'll start by penciling the first word, then fitting the next underneath, letting the letters bounce around to their best spots (see page 75 for details on bounce technique). Continue until all the words are sketched. Then, where there's some empty space on the right side, sketch a pair of shorts, which is really just two rectangles that overlap in the middle.

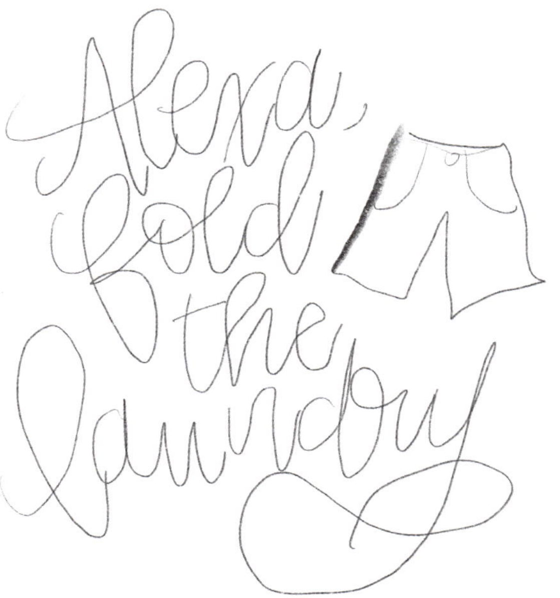

Next, use your brush pen to complete the actual brush script lettering. Trace the shorts as well and add any details you want, like a button, pockets and a waistband. Feel free to color them any shade you prefer.

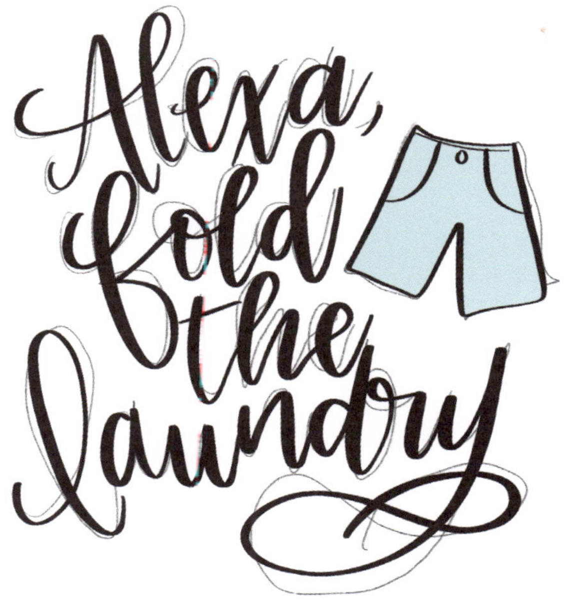

Erase your pencil lines, and you have a whimsical finished project.

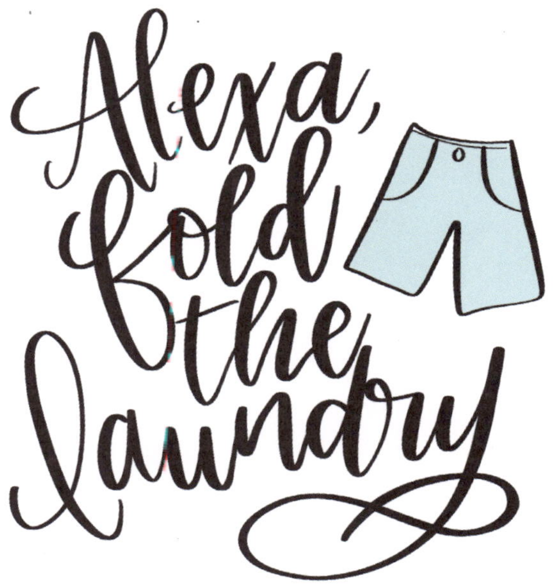

This quote on a canvas or a wooden sign would make a great sign for the laundry room! To practice the letter positioning, as well as the shorts doodle, feel free to trace the copy of my design found below. Then, try your hand at re-creating it on your own. There's a blank page with a full laundry basket at the bottom that's just waiting for your masterpiece.

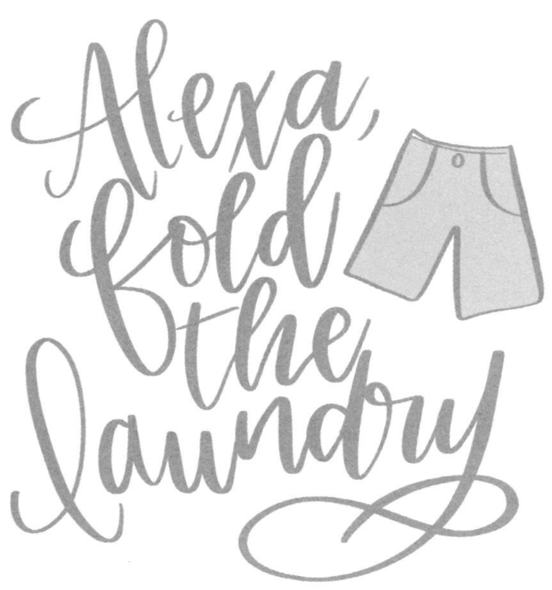

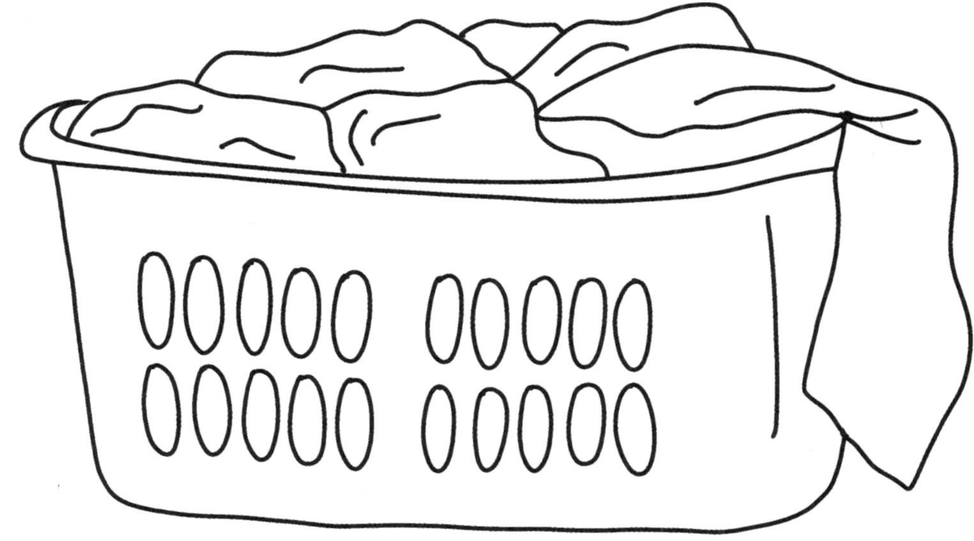

PROJECT 17

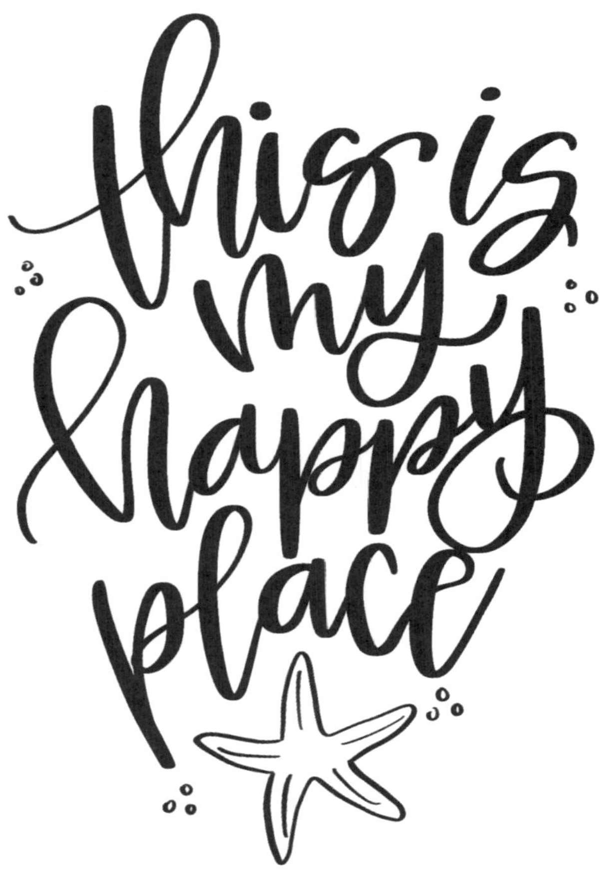

Each of us has our own "happy place." It's the space where we feel the most joy or peace, where we feel the most like ourselves. For me, it's definitely the beach. Others find their happy place in the mountains, at home, on a boat or in a favorite chair. Maybe for you, the place has less to do with location and more to do with the people who are sharing it with you. For this next quote, we're going to letter "this is my happy place" as we practice fitting our words together and using the bounce technique (page 75). I chose to illustrate my project with a little starfish to represent the beach, but you can substitute another doodle to signify your own favorite spot. When your project is finished, I think you'll know exactly where to display it.

Start by sketching "this is," then use the bounce technique to fit the word "my" underneath. Finish drawing your word positions in pencil, playing around with the letters until you're happy with how they look.

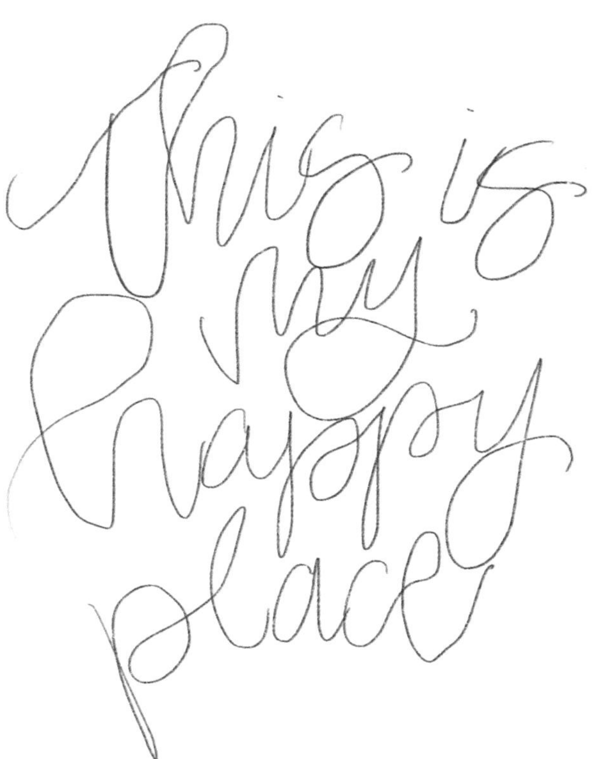

Then, use your brush pen to letter the entire phrase in brush script. Don't forget those thick downstrokes!

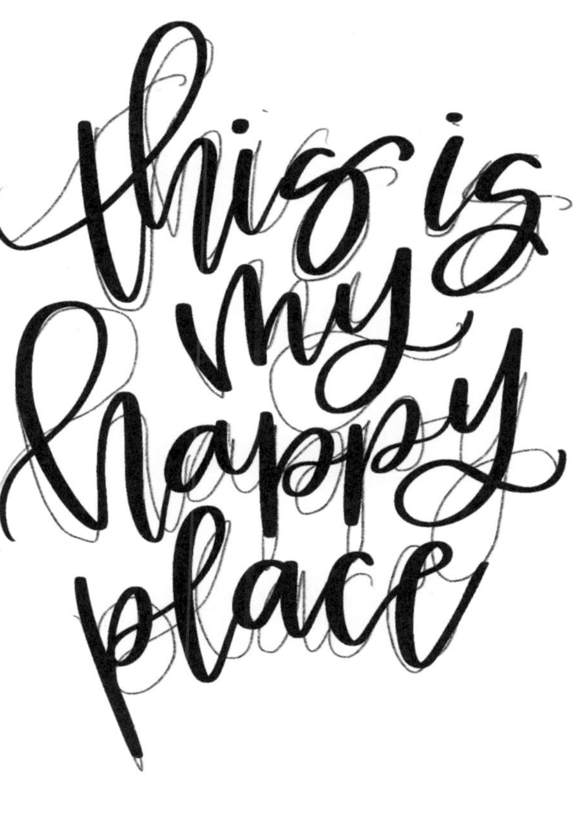

Below the phrase, there's a great opportunity to anchor the design with a little doodle that represents your happy place. Since mine is the beach, I drew a little starfish, then added a few tiny bubbles for more embellishment. You can do the same or draw anything else that's meaningful to a place you love. Erase your pencil lines and you've got a finished project. I chose not to color mine, but you can certainly add color to your doodle if you like.

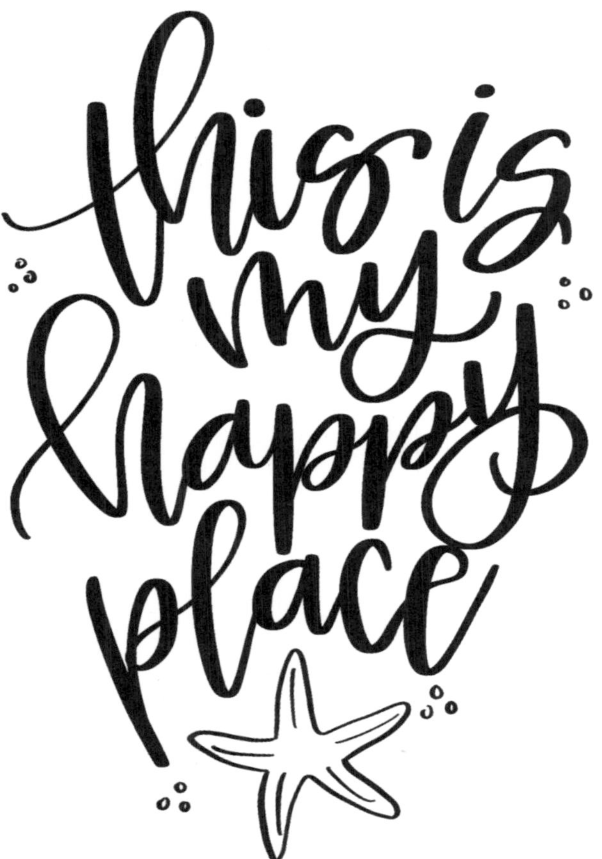

Trace the design below for some practice, then hop over to the next page and try your hand at it. This quote would also make a great sign for a beach house or wherever your happy place happens to be.

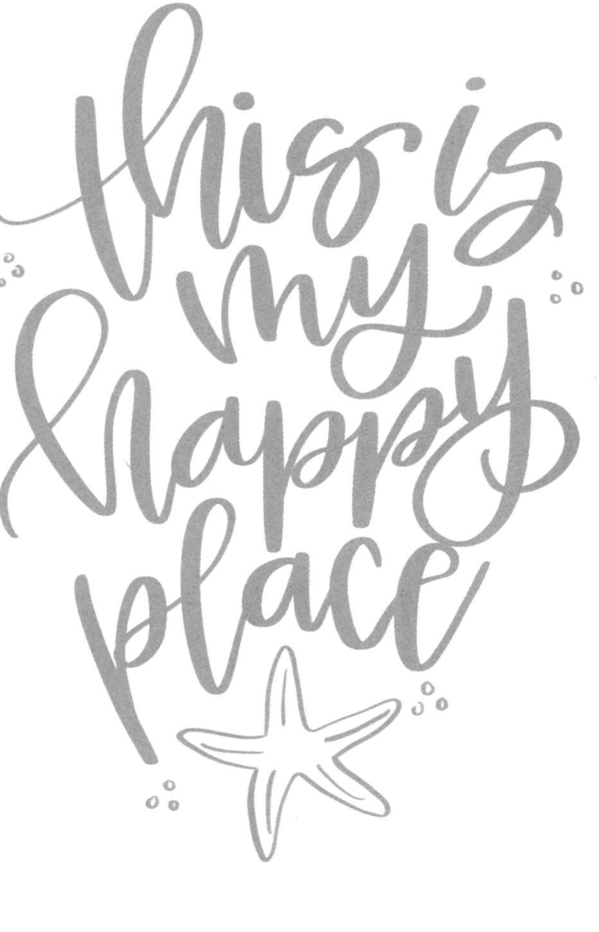

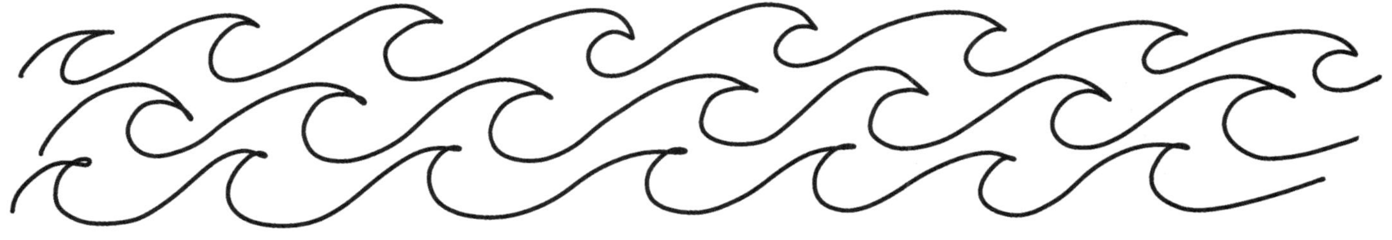

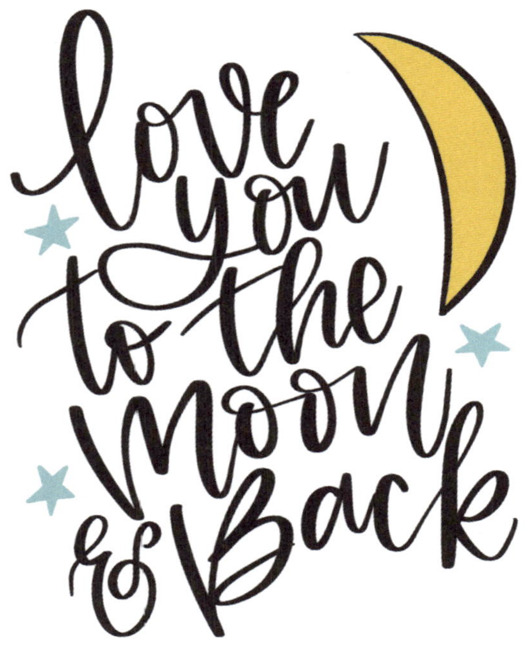

The more words a quote has, the more challenging it can be to find ways to fit them all together in a design you love. Let's try a seven-word phrase that also happens to be special to a lot of people: "love you to the moon and back." This phrase is a favorite in our family—something my son Noah and I have said to each other since he was very small. In this design, besides our lettering itself, we'll be making use of the ampersand sign, as well as a moon and a few stars for embellishments. When your project is complete, it makes a priceless gift for a special person in your life. Frame it or create it as a handmade card you can share!

Just like we did in the previous project, we'll begin by sketching word positions. I split the phrase into five lines, which I wrote on a slight angle. Using all of the forms of bounce will help you fit the letters together so that there's very little open space in between (see page 75 for details on bounce technique). Once your words are in place, you can also sketch a little moon and stars.

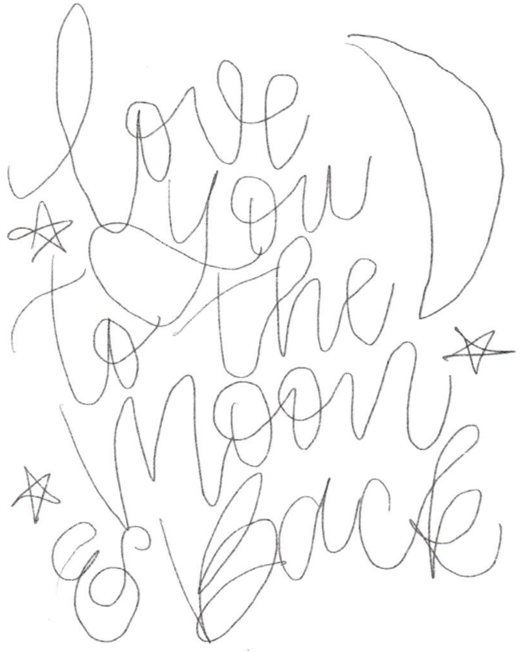

Now, it's time to break out the brush pen and letter the quote, making sure to apply pressure on every downstroke. This same technique applies to the ampersand: You'll want to treat it just like your letters. Use a black marker to trace your moon and stars or, if you prefer, you can draw the stars with a colored marker instead.

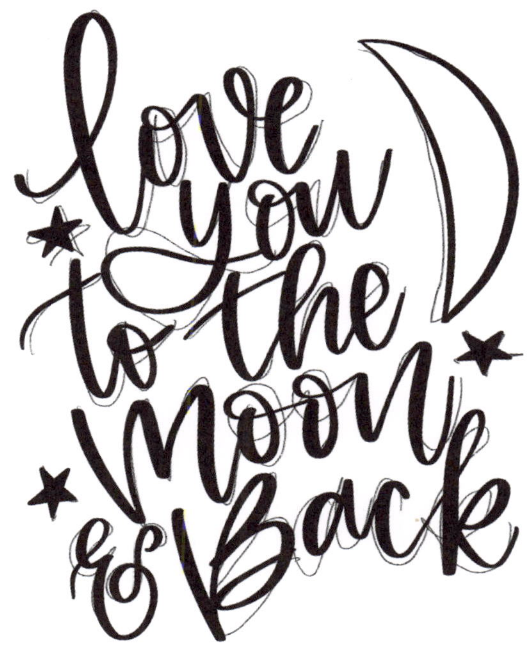

Erase your pencil marks, color the moon and your project is ready to display or give as a gift.

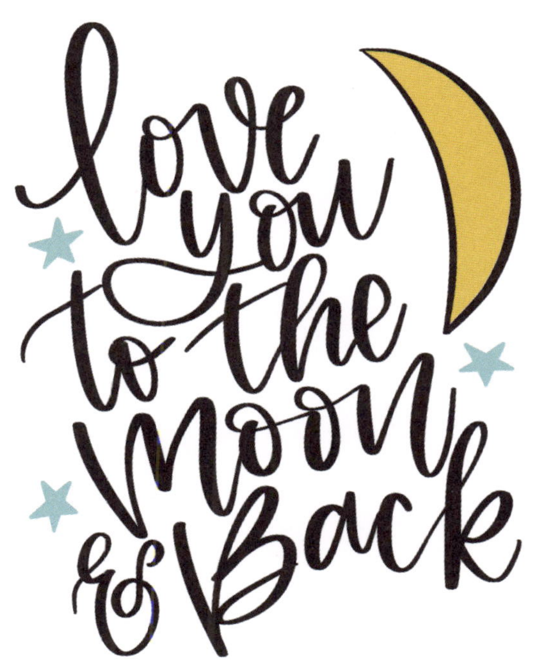

You can practice by tracing the sample below, then create your own masterpiece.

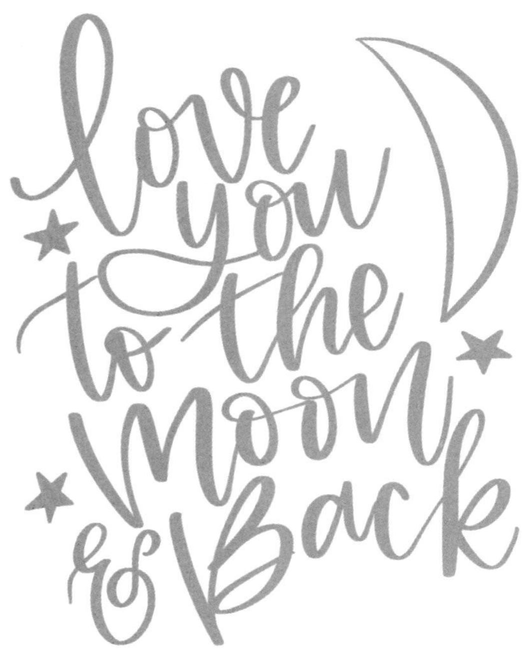

PROJECT 19

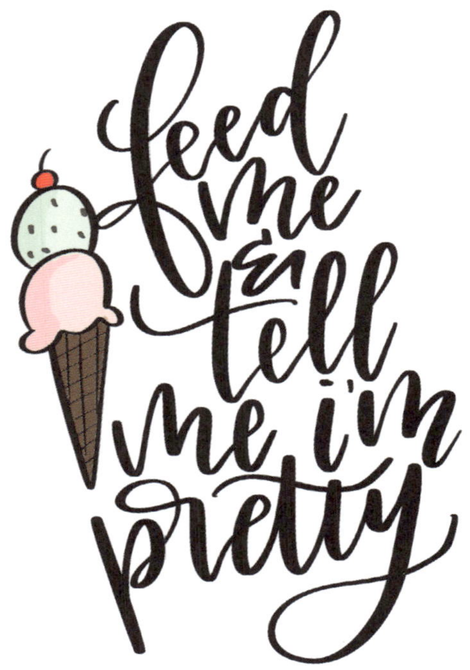

At the end of the day, all I really want are two things: to be fed and told I'm pretty. I absolutely hate cooking, so things worked out nicely when my husband decided he didn't mind it at all. We have a deal where I prepare dinner Monday through Wednesday and he cooks Thursday through Sunday. I find myself feeling so much more cheerful now on the afternoons when I know he's going to be the chef! Give me that dinner I didn't have to cook, throw a compliment on top and I'm a happy girl. This quote is fun to letter and gives us an opportunity for a cute ice cream doodle as well (which you can, of course, replace with another favorite food).

To create this whimsical design, we'll begin once again by sketching our word positions so that the quote fits together like a puzzle. Using the tilt technique and downstroke drift as you bounce your letters will help you fill all the open spaces (see page 75 for details on bounce). On the left-hand side, sketch what will be your ice cream cone: a triangle with circles on top.

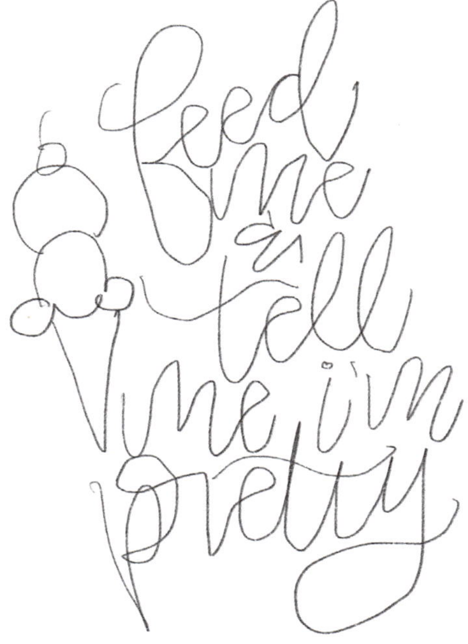

Use a brush pen to letter the phrase, always paying attention to the direction your pen is moving and applying pressure on the downstrokes. Trace your ice cream cone, adding a checkered pattern to the triangle.

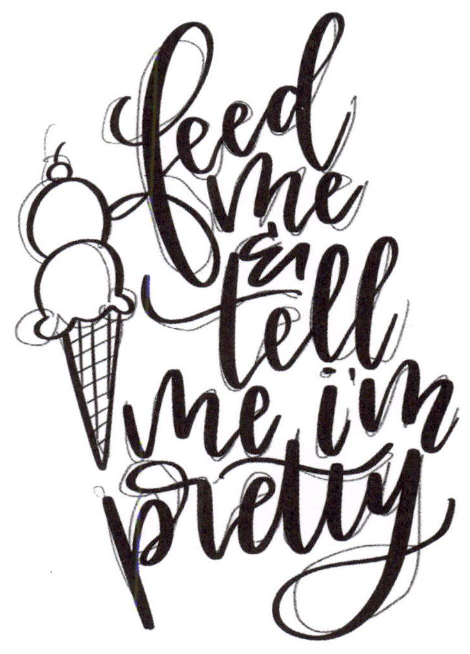

Erase your pencil marks, then color the ice cream cone, scoops and the cherry on top! Add any other details, like sprinkles or chips into the ice cream.

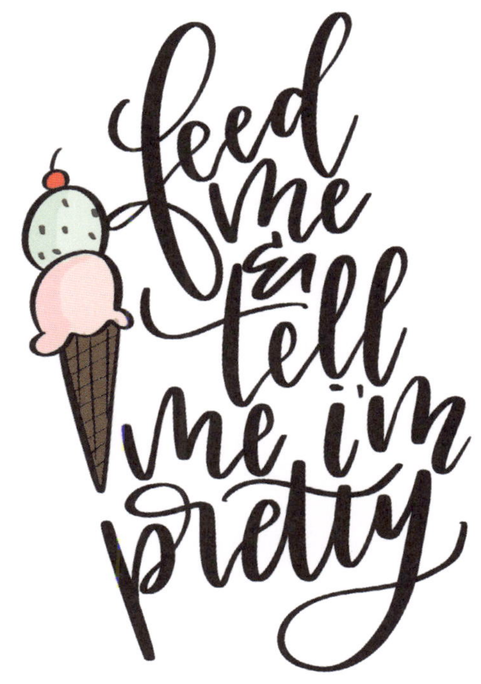

If you'd like to practice before creating your own project, trace my design below. Then, give it a try on the page with the ice cream cone along the side. As always, feel free to alter the project to make it your own.

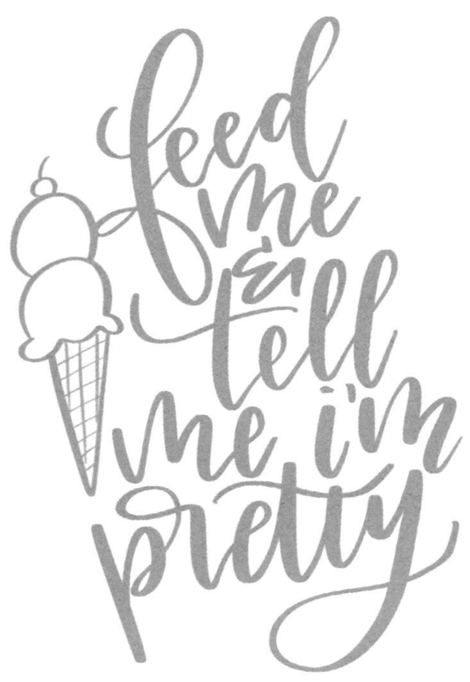

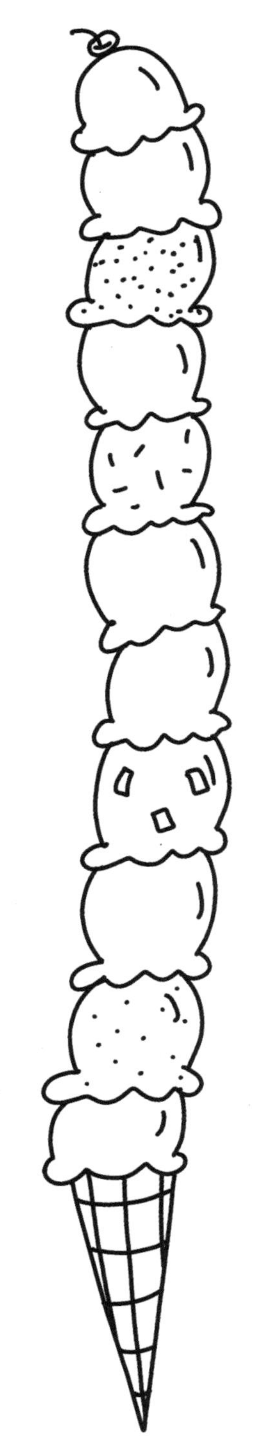

PROJECT 20

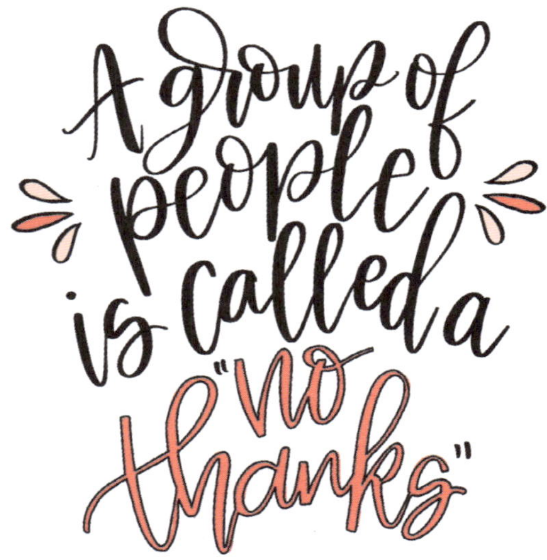

For our final project together in this book, we're going to letter a nine-word quote: "A group of people is called a no thanks." I know those of you who are fellow introverts will appreciate this one as much as I do. Extroverted readers, bear with me and create this one as a gift for an introvert you know and love. We find large groups completely draining and would rather pass up that crowded party to enjoy a quiet evening at home with our pets and a good book.

The more words we have to work with, the trickier it can be to make them all fit together well, but we're going to do it! Sketch your word positions using mine as a guide. Pay attention to what letters are shorter and longer and think about trying to fit the lines together like pieces of a puzzle. Tuck letters into the empty spaces and try to be aware of what spots would work best for letters with big ascender or descender lines.

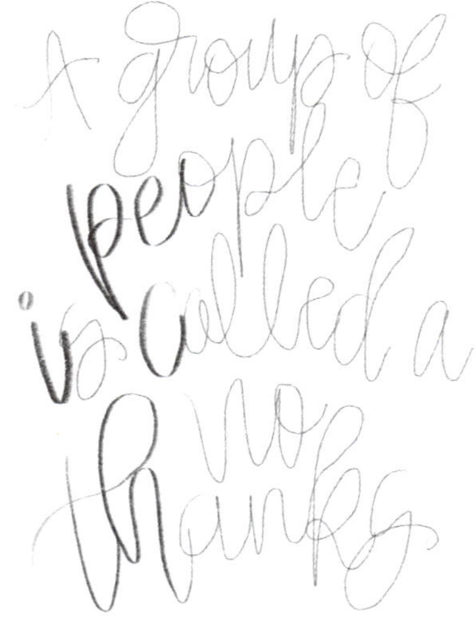

To emphasize the words "no thanks," we're going to use our outline technique, making them pop off the page more than the rest of the phrase. Use a black brush pen to letter the other words in brush script, then choose a bright colored brush pen for the "no thanks" part.

Erase the pencil lines, then carefully outline the colored lettering with a fine-tip marker (see page 73 for detail on outline technique) and then add quotation marks around "no thanks." Draw a few teardrop embellishments on either side of the design and color them to coordinate with your colored words.

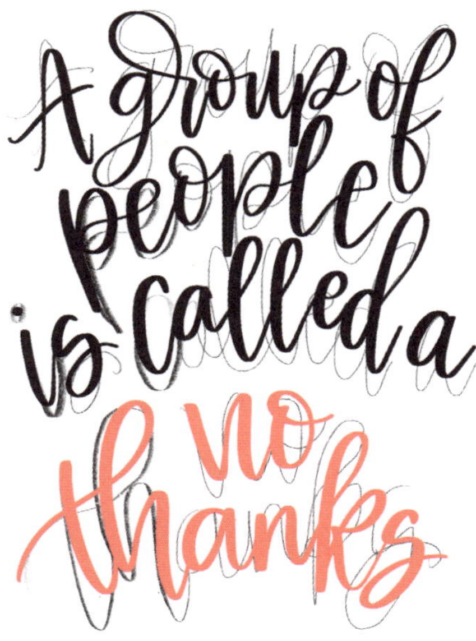

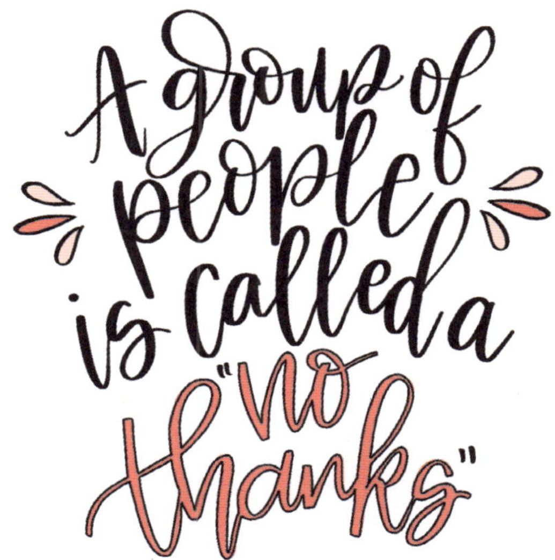

Trace the design below for a bit of practice, then create your own version on the bordered page.

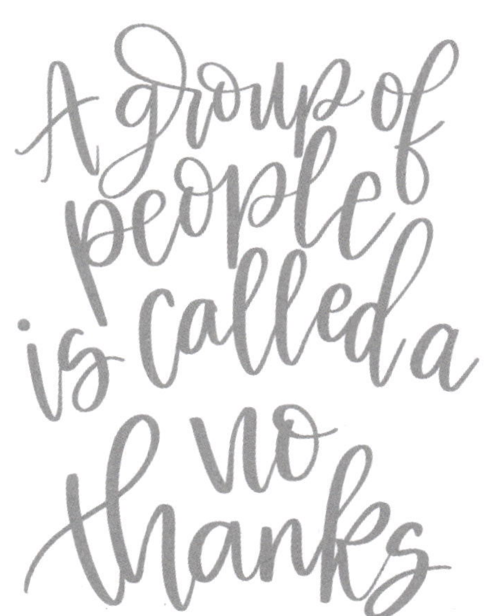

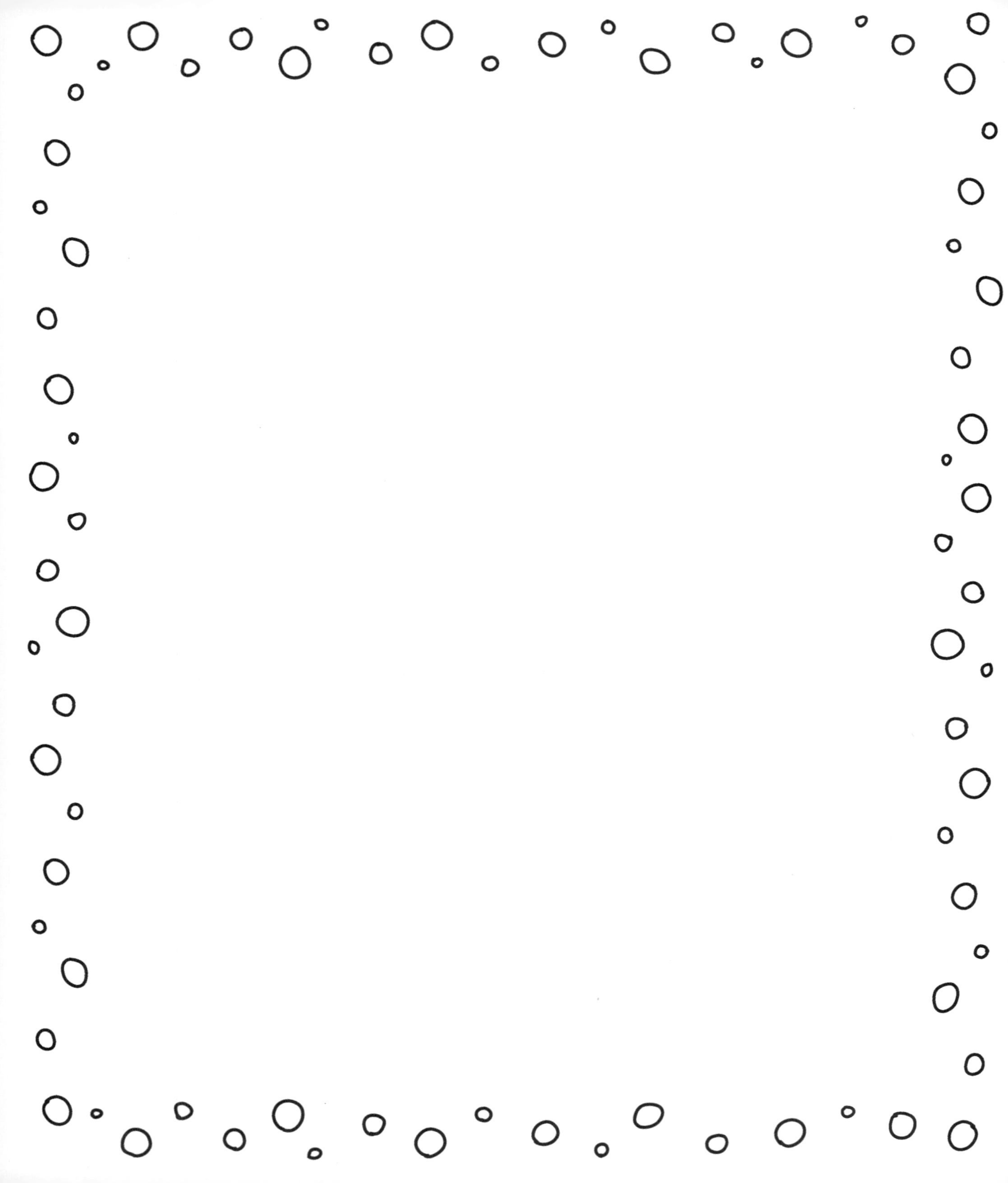

Afterword

Congratulations! You've completed twenty brush-lettering projects. Each time you traced a design or tried the lettering on your own, you embedded the technique a little more into your muscle memory. Like any skill, brush lettering becomes easier the more you do it, and you'll be able to see a lot of improvement over time if you practice regularly.

The best part is that now you can use your lettering for all kinds of creative projects, not only on paper but on all kinds of other surfaces. There's no limit to what you can create!

For more lettering instruction and inspiration, be sure to stop by amylattacreations.com. If you share images of your projects online, I'd love for you to tag me at @amylattacreations so I can celebrate with you.

About the Author

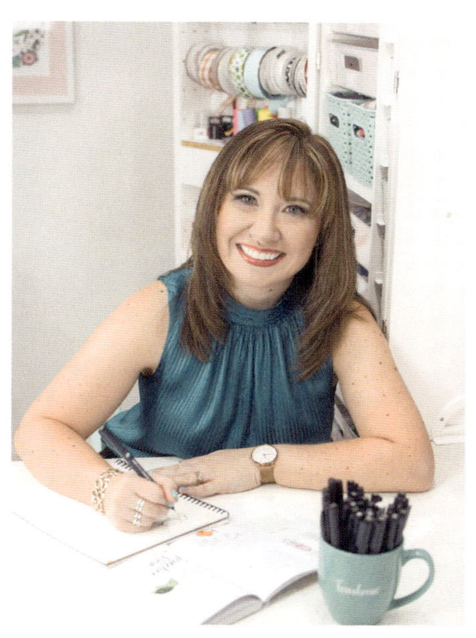

Amy Latta is passionate about helping every person she meets learn to create beautiful things. On her award-winning blog amylattacreations.com, you'll find easy-to-follow hand lettering tutorials, along with all kinds of craft and DIY projects. Amy also loves teaching in-person and virtual workshops all across the United States through Michaels Community Classroom, Pinners Conference and other venues. Another of Amy's favorite avenues for sharing creative tips is doing segments on lifestyle television shows and Pinterest TV. And, of course, you can learn from Amy by reading one or all of her five books on hand lettering, including *Hand Lettering for Relaxation*, which has sold nearly 150,000 copies as of this printing. She has also written a guided creativity journal, *Practice Makes Progress*, and a book called *Doodle Everything*, which teaches readers to draw over 400 adorable images. Amy is happiest when crafting, and when she's not covered in paint, you can find her working on hand-lettered art and professional design collaborations. Amy is a Maryland girl who runs on iced coffee and loves spending time with her husband, their two sons and their furry friends.

Acknowledgments

Will and the Page Street Team—It is a joy to partner with you. I absolutely love all that we've been able to create together. Thank you for always being willing to ask, "What do we want to do next?"

Sarah—You are not only the best editor there is, but also a kind and beautiful person inside and out. I am grateful to have you in my life.

Meg—Thank you for taking my manuscripts and illustrations and working your magic to weave them into beautiful books.

Tombow USA—Thank you for inviting me to be part of your Creator Crew and for producing brush pens and art supplies of the highest quality. It's truly my pleasure to create with your products.

Dan—I love never having to doubt that you are in my corner. Thank you for your consistent love and support and for understanding when I need to go into deadline mode. I love you more today than yesterday . . .

Noah—Yay! The book is finished, so now we have more time to play Stardew Valley! I love you, best buddy.

Nathan—Thank you for understanding when I needed to spend time working instead of playing. Now, let's get some celebratory chocolate balls and you can give me a hard time. I hear that's what best friends do.

Mom and Dad—Your support and love mean the world to me and I am so grateful for both of you. Thank you for helping me to become the person I am today and for always believing I can do and achieve anything.

Erin—Thank you for keeping the everyday tasks under control for Amy Latta Creations so that I can write more books, and for protecting me from gray sweatpants. Love you, Mocha.

Bill and Chrissy—For your friendship, enthusiasm, dog snuggles, fabulous memes and Chrissy's top-notch grilled cheeses, I am eternally grateful.

Index

A

"A group of people is called a no thanks" project, 162–164
Alcohol-based ink/markers, 5, 96
"Alexa, fold the laundry" project, 146–149
Alphabet
  brush script, in lowercase, 21–30
  brush script, uppercase, 32–41
  extended brush script, 60, 61
"ALWAYS Be kind" project, 134–137
"always give thanks" project, 113–116
Ampersand sign, 154, 155
Apple® Pencil, 7
Arrow, 98, 99
Ascender flourishes, 47–51
Ascender loop, 14, 19
Ascenders, definition, 47

B

Banners
  in "ALWAYS Be kind" project, 134–136
  in "life IS short, eat dessert first" project, 138–140
  in "practice MAKES progress" project, 88–91
  in "this IS us" project, 94–96
Bee doodle, 134–136
Blending, 82
Botanical border, 119–120
Botanicals. *See* Floral embellishments
Bounce technique, 99
  "Alexa, fold the laundry" project using, 147
  "coffee time" project using, 110
  "do more THAN just exist" project using, 123
  "Embrace THE Journey" project using, 98–99
  "every moment matters" project using, 127, 128
  explained, 75
  "feed me & tell me i'm pretty" project using, 159
  "love you to the moon & back" project using, 155
  methods for achieving, 75–76
  practice, 77–80
  "this is my happy place" project using, 150–152
  "this IS us" project using, 94
Bristol board, 6, 7, 85
Brush pens (markers)
  about, 4
  care of, 6–7
  colorful, 73
  ink types in, 5
  lifting, when writing words, 20, 44–46
  pressure applied to, 8–9
  storage of, 7
  three main types of, 6
Brush script alphabet. *See* Alphabet
Brushstrokes
  ascender loop, 14
  compound curve, 13
  descender loop, 15
  downstrokes, 8, 9, 11
  horizontal strokes, 8
  oval, 14
  overturn, 12
  underturn, 12–13
  upstrokes, 8, 9, 11
Brush technique, 8–10

C

Caliart® brush pens, 6
Capital letters
  brush script alphabet, 32–41
  extended brush script and, 60
Circle design. *See* Round designs
"coffee time" project, 109–112
Color(s) and colored pens/markers, 5, 73–74, 82
Compound curve, 13, 19
Copic® brush pens, 6
"creative minds ARE rarely tidy" project, 142–145
Crossbar, defined, 47
Crossbar flourishes, 57–59
Cupcake doodle, 138–140
Cursive handwriting, 20, 43, 44

D

Descender flourishes, 52–56
Descender loop, 15, 18, 20
Descenders, 47
Digital brush lettering, 7
"do more THAN just exist" project, 122–125
Doodles. *See also* Banners
  bee, 134–136
  cupcake, 138–140
  ice cream, 159–160
  shorts, 147
  starfish, 150, 152
  stars and moon, 154–156
Dots, 82
Downstroke, 8, 9, 12, 13, 60
Downstroke drift, 76, 85, 94, 127, 159
Drop shadows, 81
Dye/water-based brush pens, 6

E

Embellishments. *See also* Doodles
  flowers and leaves, 105–107, 130–132
  teardrop, 123, 128, 163
"Embrace THE Journey" project, 98–101
"every moment matters" project, 126–129
Extended brush script, 60–72
  alphabet, 61
  explained, 60
  practice, 62–69, 71–72
  words, 70

F

"feed me & tell me i'm pretty" project, 158–161
Finished examples, 83
Floral border, 119–120
Floral embellishments
  in "IT IS Well With MY Soul" project, 105–107
  in "you are my favorite person" project, 130–132
Flourishes, 47–59
  ascender, 47–51
  crossbar, 57–59
  descender, 52–56
  projects using, 114, 123–124, 130
Fudenosuke brush pens, 6, 60, 81

H

Highlights, 81
Horizontal lines/strokes, 8, 60
Hot press watercolor paper, 6, 7
House image, "this is us" lettering inside, 93–96

I

Ice cream cone doodle, 158–159
Inks
  alcohol-based, 5
  water-based, 5
In-letter bounce, 75, 99
iPad®, 7
"IT IS Well WITH MY Soul" project, 105–108

J

"joy," 73–74

L

Laser printed paper, 6
Layering, with water-based versus alcohol-based inks, 5
Leaves, 105–107, 114–115, 119, 131

Letters
bounce added within, 75–76, 99
connecting, 43–46
creating the amount of space between, 60
extended brush, 61–69
lowercase brush script, 21–30
uppercase brush script, 32–41
"life IS short, eat dessert first" project, 138–141
"live a life you love" project, 84–87
"love you to the moon & back" project, 154–157
Lowercase letters
brush script alphabet, 21–30
extended brush script, 61–69

N
"no rain, no flowers" project, 117–121
Numbers, 30

O
Outlined brush script
"A group of people is called 'no thanks'" project using, 163
"creative minds ARE rarely tidy" project using, 143
explained, 73–74
"THE best IS yet TO come" project using, 102–103, 143
Oval shape, creating letters from, 14, 18
Overturn, 12, 13

P
Papers
brush pen protection and, 6–7
water-based ink for, 5
Pencil sketches, 83
Permanent (alcohol-based) ink, 5, 6
Pigment-based brush pens, 6
Pigment/water-based brush pens, 6
Practice
adding bounce, 76–80
ascender flourishes, 48–51
brush script alphabet, lower case, 21–30
brush script alphabet, upper case, 32–41
connecting letters, 46
crossbar flourishes, 57–59
descender flourishes, 52–56
eight basic brushstrokes, 8, 9–10, 12, 13, 14, 15–17
extended brush script, 62–69, 71–72
"practice MAKES progress" project, 89–92
Printer paper, 6
Prismacolor® brush pens, 6
Procreate®, 7
Projects
"A group of people is called a no thanks," 162–164
"Alexa, fold the laundry," 146–149
"ALWAYS Be kind," 134–137
"always give thanks," 113–116
"coffee time," 109–112
"creative minds ARE rarely tidy," 142–145
"do more THAN just exist," 122–125
"Embrace THE Journey," 98–101
"every moment matters," 126–129
"feed me & tell me i'm pretty," 158–161
"IT IS Well WITH MY Soul," 105–108
"life IS short, eat dessert first," 138–141
"live a life you love," 84–87
"love you to the moon & back," 154–157
"no rain, no flowers," 117–121
"practice MAKES progress," 89–92
"THE best IS yet TO come," 102
"this is my happy place," 150–153
"this IS us," 93–97
"you are my favorite person," 130–132

R
Raindrop shape, "no rain, no flowers" lettering within, 117–120
Rectangle shape
"creative minds are rarely tidy" lettering in, 142–143
"live a life you love" lettering in, 85–86
Retracing lines, 20, 43–44
Round designs
"always give thanks" project using, 113–115
"coffee time" project using, 109–111
"every moment matters" project using, 126–129
"you are my favorite person" project using, 130–132

S
Shadows, 81
Shorts doodle, 150–152
Spectrum Noir™ brush pens, 6
Starfish doodle, 150–152
Stars and moon doodle, 155–156
Storage, of brush pens, 7
Surfaces, brush pen protection and, 6–7

T
Teardrop embellishments, 123, 128, 163
Teardrop shape, "no rain, no flowers" lettering in, 117–120
Texture, adding dots to letters for, 82
"t" flourishes, 57–59
"THE best IS yet TO come" project, 102–104
Thick lines, 8
Thin lines, 8
"this is my happy place" project, 150–153
"this IS us" project, 93–97
Tilt technique, 76, 127, 159
Tombow ABT PRO Alcohol-Based Markers, 6, 85
Tombow Dual Brush Pens, 6
Tombow® Fudenosuke pens, 6, 60, 81
Tombow MONO Drawing Pen, 73, 94
Traceable images, 83, 85, 86, 91, 96, 100, 103, 107, 111, 115, 120, 124, 128, 132, 140, 144, 148, 152, 156, 160, 163
Triangle shape, "do more THAN just exist" lettering in, 122–124

U
Underturn, 12–13, 18, 20
Upstrokes, 8, 9, 12, 13

W
Washable inks, 5
Water-based pens/markers, 5, 6
Watercolor paper, 6, 7
Watercolor, pens/markers that are best for, 6
White gel pen, 81, 82
Words
adding bounce within, 76
extended brush script, 60, 70–72
lifting the pen while writing, 20, 43, 44–46
outlined, 73–74
retracing lines while writing, 43, 44

Y
"you are my favorite person" project, 130–132